VISUAL QUICKSTART GUIDE

ADOBE ACROBAT 6

FOR WINDOWS AND MACINTOSH

Jennifer Alspach

Peachpit Press

Visual QuickStart Guide

Adobe Acrobat 6 for Windows and Macintosh

Jennifer Alspach

Peachpit Press

1249 Eighth Street
Berkeley, CA 94710
510/524-2178
800/283-9444
510/524-2221 (fax)
Find us on the World Wide Web at: www.peachpit.com
To report errors, please send a note to errata@peachpit.com

Peachpit Press is a division of Pearson Education

Editor: Becky Morgan
Production Coordinator: Becky Winter
Copyeditor: Kate McKinley
Technical Editor: John Deubert
Compositor: Jerry Ballew
Indexer: Joy Dean Lee
Cover Design: The Visual Group

ISBN 0-321-20546-4

9 8 7 6 5 4 3 2 1

♻ Printed on recycled paper

Printed and bound in the United States of America

Dedication

This book is dedicated to Linus and Pyro who shared their love and their lives.

Acknowledgments

Even though this book has my name all over it, many people helped in getting it from paper to press.

Most importantly I'd like to thank Ted Alspach. His confidence and encouragement guide me through all that I do. He is truly my inspiration.

Many thank yous to Gage and Dakota who put up with my rantings and ravings as I was finishing up this book. They learned my mantra "Just one more chapter."

Thanks go out to my mom and dad who always encouraged me to do the best I can do and still be happy.

I'll always be thankful to my support group of friends: Becky Dutcher, Julie Garrison, Sue Ingram, Tracey Shobert, Christie Brown, Melanie Rejebian, and Karen Kennedy. They are the best group of friends anyone could have!

The Acrobat team at Adobe, which has revolutionized the way that documents are distributed around the world.

Becky Morgan, my extraordinary editor at Peachpit Press. She took these words and ideas and helped mold them into a wonderful, informative piece of work.

Thanks to Becky Winter for her production finesse and commitment to making this major update look so good.

Many thanks to John Deubert, technical editor who went above and beyond the call of duty.

Last but not least, thanks to everyone at Peachpit Press who helped move this book along and get it into your hands.

TABLE OF CONTENTS

ADOBE
READER BASICS

Adobe's Portable Document Format (PDF) file format is truly amazing: It lets you read any electronic document on almost any computer system. Anyone with the free Adobe Reader software can open and view a document converted to a PDF, and it will look exactly the way it did in the original authoring program. It doesn't matter how the document was originally created.

The following pages provide an overview of Adobe Reader. It's a great way to grasp what this software can do for you.

Downloading Adobe Reader

Most people download the free Adobe Reader program so they can view the many PDF files available on the World Wide Web. Most Web sites that include PDF files also provide a link to download Reader, but you can always find it on Adobe's Web site.

To download Adobe Reader from Adobe's Web site:

1. Using your Web browser, go to the Adobe Web site (www.adobe.com).

2. On the home page, click "Acrobat products" under the Products menu.

3. On the Acrobat page, click the Get Adobe Reader link (**Figure 1.1**). This brings up the Download page.

4. Following the instructions provided on the site, choosing your language, platform, and connection speed; then click the Download button (**Figure 1.2**).

5. Choose a location to download to.

   Once the file has finished downloading, your browser will automatically decompress it (Macintosh only) and you'll see the Adobe Reader Installer icon in the specified location (**Figure 1.3**).

Figure 1.1 Click the Get Adobe Reader icon.

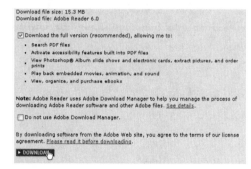

Figure 1.2 Choose a language, platform, and connection speed, then click the Download button.

Figure 1.3 Once the download is finished, you'll see the Adobe Reader Installer icon.

✔ Tips

■ On the Mac, Adobe uses a Web-based installer. Clicking the Download button sends
a small application to your computer,
which you later run outside the browser.
(See "Installing Adobe Reader" on the
next page.)

■ Most of the time, the people who create
and distribute Acrobat PDF documents
provide Adobe Reader as well. If you
download a PDF file from a Web page,
you're likely to find a link to a downloadable version of Adobe Reader. The link is
usually identified by the icon (or "badge,"
as Adobe calls it) shown in Figure 1.1.
Likewise, if your PDF file came on a
CD-ROM, there's probably a copy of
Adobe Reader on the disc.

■ Adobe Reader now includes Acrobat
eBook Reader 2.2 (discussed in Chapter 3,
"Adobe eBook Reader").

Installing Adobe Reader

The installation procedure for Adobe Reader varies, depending on where the installer came from and on which platform you're installing Reader. All Windows users and many Mac users will follow a *disk-based* procedure, meaning the complete installer is either supplied on a CD-ROM or downloaded from the Web to the user's hard disk. Some Mac users will employ *Web-based* installation (Windows users will not be given this choice), which uses a small program downloaded from Adobe's Web site to download the complete Adobe Reader software.

Figure 1.4 The Adobe Reader 6.0 Setup screen begins the installation process.

To install Adobe Reader (Windows):

1. Find the Adobe Reader Installer icon on the desktop and double-click it to launch the installation process.

2. The Adobe Reader 6.0 Setup screen (**Figure 1.4**) will prompt you through the installation process. Click Next to continue.

3. The installer automatically selects a location on your hard drive in which to install Reader. The default directory path is displayed in the Destination Folder window (**Figure 1.5**). If the default directory is correct, click Next. To change the location, click the Change Destination Folder button and navigate to your preferred directory.

   At this point Adobe Reader will begin to install itself. A status bar will pop up to track the installation's progress (**Figure 1.6**). You can stop the process at any time by clicking Cancel.

4. Once installation is complete, a dialog box will ask if you want to restart Windows. Select this option and click Finish. The installer will then quit and Windows will restart.

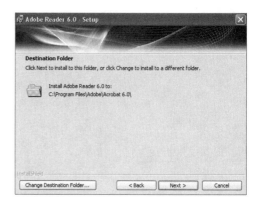

Figure 1.5 Reader is installed to a default directory location.

Figure 1.6 You can watch the progress bar to see how the installation is going.

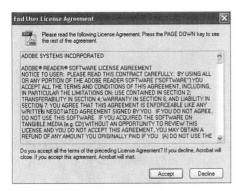

Figure 1.7 You must accept the End User License Agreement before you can use Reader.

Figure 1.8 The Adobe Download Manager appears and starts the download process.

Figure 1.9 The Disk Copy Progress window shows the progress of the rest of the installation.

Figure 1.10 Once the files are downloaded and installed, you'll see an Adobe Reader 6.0 folder.

5. Verify that Adobe Reader has been installed properly by opening its destination directory. There you should find the Adobe Reader 6.0 application, PrintMe Internet Printing folder, and ReadMe.html file).

The first time you launch Reader, the End User License Agreement will appear (**Figure 1.7**). You must accept the agreement before you can use Reader.

To install Adobe Reader (Macintosh):

1. Find the Adobe Reader Installer icon and double-click it to launch the installation process.

The Adobe Download Manager appears and starts downloading Reader (**Figure 1.8**). The Adobe Download Manager shows the progress and destination of the downloaded file.

When the download is complete, Disk Copy automatically takes over, and Disk Copy Progress displays the status of the rest of the installation (**Figure 1.9**).

2. After Disk Copy is done, you'll see the Adobe Reader folder on your desktop (**Figure 1.10**). To check that Reader was installed properly, open the folder. Inside you should find the Adobe Reader 6.0 application, the ReadMe.html document, and the PrintMe Internet Printing folder (**Figure 1.11**).

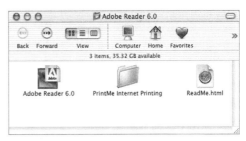

Figure 1.11 Check that Reader was installed properly by opening the Adobe Reader 6.0 folder.

INSTALLING ADOBE READER

The Adobe Reader Screen

The Adobe Reader's modular, customizable interface is essentially the same as Acrobat's, but with a more limited tool set (**Figure 1.12**). Most of the tools and panes you see on the screen can be separated from their neighbors, moved to different parts of the screen, combined in groups as you see fit, or banished altogether.

Running across the top of the application window is the menu bar, containing the drop-down menus. Just below the menu bar are the toolbars, which give you quick access to the most commonly used commands for file manipulation, viewing, and navigation.

The document window is divided into two panes (**Figure 1.13**). The Navigation pane, along the left-hand side of the window, provides sophisticated controls for finding your way through a PDF document. Most of the screen is occupied by the Document pane, which contains the file itself. Clicking on the small right-pointing arrow in the upper-right corner of the Document pane brings up a menu (**Figure 1.14**) that provides quick access to detailed information about your document, as well as the Preferences dialog box. The status bar along the bottom of the Document pane (**Figure 1.15**) summarizes data about the currently active document and offers alternative methods for displaying your document.

Finally, there are five panes—Bookmarks, Signatures, Layers, Pages, and Articles—that are the most flexible elements of the Reader interface. Each pane has its own pop-up menu of options pertaining to it, and can be pulled out of the Navigation pane and placed anywhere on the screen.

Figure 1.12 The Adobe Reader toolbars.

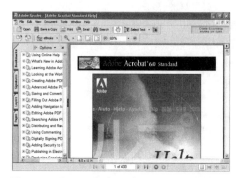

Figure 1.13 On any platform, the Document and Navigation panes fill the bulk of the Reader window.

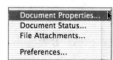

Figure 1.14 This pop-out menu in the Document pane can take you right to the Preferences dialog box.

Figure 1.15 The status bar below the Document pane holds some basic information and tools.

✓ Basic
✓ File
✓ Navigation
✓ Rotate View
✓ Tasks
✓ Zoom

Properties Bar   ⌘E

✓ Tool Button Labels
Hide Toolbars   F8
Dock All Toolbars   ⌥⌘D
Reset Toolbars
Lock Toolbars

Figure 1.16 There are six toolbars for you to show or hide.

The Toolbars

What appears to be a single toolbar is actually a collection of toolbars—Basic, File, Navigation, Rotate View, Tasks, and Zoom—that you can hide or show as you desire (**Figure 1.16**).

The toolbars (**Figures 1.17** through **1.22**) are pretty darn easy to use: Simply click the button for the tool you want to use. To send a file to the printer, for instance, just click the Print button to open the Print dialog box. Some buttons are hiding multiple tools behind them. These are revealed when you click the top-level, visible button.

(continues on next page)

Figure 1.17 The Basic toolbar contains basic tools.

Figure 1.18 Go to the File toolbar for quick file management.

Figure 1.19 The Navigation toolbar lets you sail through a document.

Figure 1.20 The Rotate toolbar does exactly what it promises.

Figure 1.21 The Tasks toolbar is for more complicated activities.

Figure 1.22 The tools on the Zoom toolbar let you increase or decrease magnification.

✔ Tips

- If you don't like the way the toolbars are arranged, change 'em around! Position the mouse pointer over the vertical separator bar on the left side of the toolbar grouping you want to move, then drag the toolbar to its new position. Any toolbars beneath the one you've moved will step politely out of the way to accommodate the newcomer.

- Although you can move toolbars around the screen, you can't change their shape or orientation.

- Can't remember what a particular toolbar button does? Thanks to the magic of tool tips, any button will tell you its name—just let the mouse pointer hover over it for a second or two (**Figure 1.23**).

To hide and show individual toolbars:

1. Choose Toolbars from the View menu. A submenu pops out, showing a list of all of the available toolbars (**Figure 1.24**). Currently visible toolbars have a checkmark by their names.

or

Right-click (Windows) or Control-click (Mac) any individual toolbar. A contextual menu will appear, listing all of the toolbars.

2. To hide a toolbar, click its checked name in the Toolbars submenu or contextual menu. To display a hidden toolbar, click its unchecked name.

✔ Tip

- Press F8 to quickly show or hide all of the toolbars at once.

Figure 1.23 A tool tip pops up to identify the object your mouse is hovering over.

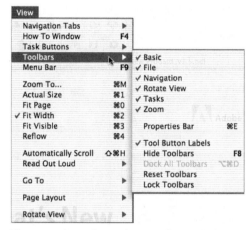

Figure 1.24 The Toolbars submenu tells you which toolbars are visible.

THE TOOLBARS

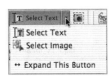

Figure 1.25 More tools are hiding beneath these arrows in the toolbars.

Figure 1.26 Choose Expand This Button and guess what happens.

Some toolbars keep a few command buttons tucked away out of sight. The key to unlocking these secret commands is the More Tools feature, marked by a minuscule downward-pointing arrow to the right of certain toolbar buttons (**Figure 1.25**).

To display and rehide hidden toolbar buttons:

1. Click a More Tools arrow to see a menu of that toolbar's hidden commands. Choose an item from the menu to activate the command.

2. Choose Expand This Button at the bottom of the More Tools menu, to add the hidden buttons to the toolbar (**Figure 1.26**).
   The More Tools button transforms into the Collapse button, marked by a left-pointing arrow, to indicate that the button has been expanded.

3. To tuck away a toolbar's expanded buttons, click its Collapse arrow. The toolbar returns to its default state.

The Reader Menus

Adobe Reader's pull-down menus—File, Edit, View, Document, Tools, Window, and Help—live in the menu bar running along the top of the application window. On the Macintosh, there is an additional menu called Adobe Reader (**Figure 1.27**). To access a menu's commands, simply click the menu, then move the mouse to the function you want.

✔ Tip

■ Press F9 to show or hide the menu bar.

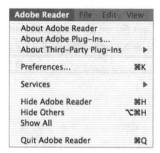

Figure 1.27 The Adobe Reader menu in Macintosh offers information about Reader and your installed plug-ins, access to Preferences, and other services.

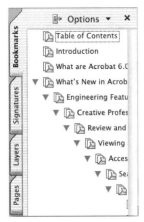

Figure 1.28 Panes in the Navigation pane help you find your way around a Reader document.

The Reader Panes

The panes are mini-windows that assist you in finding your way through a PDF document—Bookmarks, Signatures, Layers, Pages, and Articles. By default, the panes are "docked" in the Navigation pane of the document window, but the pane can be moved, resized, and grouped. When they're in the Navigation pane, you can see the tabs of all panes (which is why Adobe refers to them as "tabbed panes"), but only the top pane's contents are visible (**Figure 1.28**). Just click a tab to see the contents of another pane.

You can pull a tabbed pane out of the Navigation pane by clicking its tab and dragging it anywhere on the screen. Then it's called a "floating panel" and can be moved freely around the screen by dragging its label. You can also group floating panels together by dragging the tab of one into the window of another. The Articles pane is a floating panel by default (choose View > Navigation Tabs > Articles to see it) but you can dock it in the Navigation pane or pull other panes out to join it.

To show or hide the Navigation pane:

1. If the Navigation pane is hidden, choose View > Navigation Tabs > Open Navigation Pane.

2. To hide the open Navigation pane, choose View > Navigation Tabs > Close Navigation Pane.

(continues on next page)

THE READER PANES

✔ Tips

- You can also click the double arrow in the bottom-left corner of the Document pane to open or close the Navigation pane. Or you can show, hide, or resize the Navigation Pane by dragging its right edge with the mouse.

- Don't confuse the Navigation pane with the navigation tools in the status bar at the bottom of the Document pane. Those can't be removed or hidden. (See the following section for more about the status bar.)

To show or hide a pane:

1. To show a pane, choose it from the Navigation Tabs submenu of the View menu. A checkmark will appear next to its name and it will become visible.

2. To hide a tabbed pane, choose it from the Navigation Tabs submenu of the View menu. The checkmark will disappear from its name and only the tab will be visible.

   or

   To hide a floating pane, click the close box in the upper-right corner (upper-left corner for Macs) of its window (**Figure 1.29**).

Figure 1.29 Click the close box in the upper-right (Windows) or upper-left (Macintosh) corner to close the floating window.

The Status Bar

Nestled along the bottom of the Document pane, the status bar (**Figure 1.30**) provides yet another set of controls for making your way through a PDF file. Their position along the bottom of the Acrobat interface makes these controls most intuitive when you're just reading straight through a PDF document: You can get at them without having to reach across the page. These controls will be covered later in the chapter.

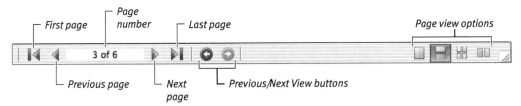

Figure 1.30 The status bar holds navigational controls.

Opening a PDF File

The first step in reading any document is to open it. This procedure is pretty much the same in Adobe Reader as in other standard applications.

To open an existing PDF file:

◆ Choose Open from the File menu (Ctrl+O/Command+O). This launches the Open dialog box, where you can select your PDF document and click the Open button (**Figure 1.31**).

   or

   Double-click the PDF file's icon (**Figure 1.32**) or drag the PDF file's icon on top of the Adobe Reader icon on your desktop. This will open the file in Reader.

✔ Tip

■ *Mac only:* If your PDF file doesn't appear in the Open dialog box, choose All Files from the Show pop-up menu (**Figure 1.33**). Files of every kind—whether identified as belonging to Acrobat or not—will appear in the dialog box and be available to open.

To close a PDF file:

◆ Choose Close from the File menu (Ctrl+W/Command+W).

   or

   Click the close box in the upper-right corner (upper-left corner on Macs) of the document window.

To close all open documents at once:

◆ Choose Close All from the Window menu (Ctrl+Alt+W/Option+Command+W).

Because Adobe Reader can't actually alter the PDF documents, it will never save your changes. When you close a file, the program simply sweeps it from your screen.

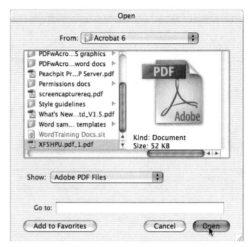

Figure 1.31 Choose the document to open in the Open dialog box.

Figure 1.32 Double-click a file's icon to open it.

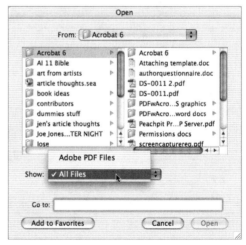

Figure 1.33 Choose Show All Files in the Open dialog box to display unidentified PDF files.

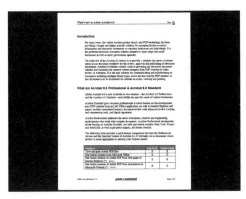

Figure 1.34 In Full Screen mode, your document stands alone.

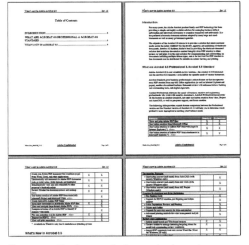

Figure 1.35 Continuous-Facing mode shows two pages across and as many as necessary down.

✔ **Tip**

■ You can set page display options for Full Screen mode in the Full Screen area of the Preferences dialog box.

Viewing a PDF File

Adobe Reader gives you some general options for viewing a PDF file: You can view just the document itself without the toolbar and menus, and you can choose between single-page and multiple-page views.

To view the document only:

1. Choose Full Screen from the Window menu (Ctrl+L/Command+L).

   Everything but the currently open document will be hidden, including the Reader menu bar and any application windows (**Figure 1.34**).

2. To exit Full Screen mode, press the Esc key (or Ctrl+L/Command+L). The document will then be restored to its previous display, with all the menus, windows, and toolbars.

To view a single page:

◆ Choose View > Page Layout > Single Page, or click the Single Page button in the status bar.

   The Document pane will display one page at a time.

To view continuous pages:

◆ Choose View > Page Layout > Continuous, or click the Continuous button in the status bar.

   The Document pane will display all the pages in a vertical line as you scroll, rather than flipping from one page to the next.

To view continuous facing pages:

◆ Choose View > Page Layout > Continuous-Facing.

   The Document pane will display multiple successive pages in two-page spreads across the document window (**Figure 1.35**).

Using Zoom

Looking at an entire page at once is very convenient for some tasks, but the resulting small text size may make it difficult to read the contents of the page (see Figure 1.34). Fortunately, Adobe Reader offers a number of zoom options to let you quickly swoop into, and back away from, your document. As if there weren't already enough ways to zoom in or out of a document, Adobe has added another one to the mix. In addition to the many tools, buttons, and menus for zooming in previous versions, Acrobat 6 and Reader include a cool new Dynamic Zoom tool that changes the magnification as you move your mouse.

To magnify a document:

◆ Click the Zoom In button on the Zoom toolbar (**Figure 1.36**). The magnification increases by a preset amount.

   or

   Choose Tools > Zoom > Zoom In to select the Zoom In tool. Click in the document to zoom in by a preset amount.

To reduce a document:

◆ Click the Zoom Out button on the Zoom toolbar to decrease magnification by a preset amount.

   or

   Choose Tools > Zoom > Zoom Out to select the Zoom Out tool. Click in the document to zoom out by a preset amount.

✔ Tip

■ To zoom out from a specific point, click the Zoom Out tool in the toolbar and click in the Document pane. Or, with the Zoom In tool selected, Alt/Option-click to zoom out by a preset amount or right-click/Control-click for a contextual menu of available magnifications.

Figure 1.36 The Zoom toolbar holds the Zoom In and Zoom Out buttons.

Figure 1.37 Click the Zoom In tool and you'll be able to enlarge your view of the document.

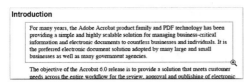

Figure 1.38 Drag a marquee with the Zoom In tool to define an area for enlargement.

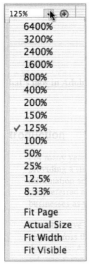

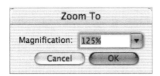

Figure 1.39 The magnification drop-down menu presents all your preset choices.

Figure 1.40 Enter your chosen magnification amount in the Zoom To dialog box.

To define the boundaries of the zoomed area:

1. Click the Zoom In tool in the Zoom toolbar (**Figure 1.37**).

2. Click and drag your mouse to make a marquee (a dashed-line rectangle) around the area you want to zoom in on (**Figure 1.38**). When you release the mouse button, the selected area will fill the document window.

To zoom to a specific magnification:

◆ Click the downward arrow next to the magnification indicator in the Zoom toolbar (**Figure 1.39**), then select a preset zoom level from the menu that appears.

   or

   While using either zoom tool, right-click/Control-click to bring up a contextual menu of the preset magnification choices.

   or

   Select Zoom To from the View menu (Ctrl+M/Command+M). In the Zoom To dialog box (**Figure 1.40**), enter the magnification percentage you want or select a preset magnification from the pop-up menu, and click OK.

   The document will be displayed at the magnification you specified.

(continues on next page)

USING ZOOM

✔ Tip

- You can also zoom to a magnification relative to the document or window size.

- ◆ Actual Size (Ctrl+1/Command+1) shows the document at 100 percent magnification.

- ◆ Fit Page (Ctrl+0/Command+0) resizes the document so that its edges just fit in the Document pane.

- ◆ Fit Width (Ctrl+2/Command+2) resizes the document so that its full width fills the Document pane.

- ◆ Fit Visible (Ctrl+3/Command+3) resizes the page so that all of its text and graphics fill the Document pane, cutting out blank margin space.

To use the Dynamic Zoom tool:

1. Click the Dynamic Zoom tool in the Zoom toolbar (**Figure 1.41**).

2. Click and drag diagonally upward to zoom in, downward to zoom out.

   When you release the mouse, your document will stay at the magnification you chose.

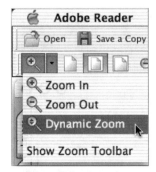

Figure 1.41 The Dynamic Zoom tool lives with Zoom In and Zoom Out in the Zoom toolbar.

USING ZOOM

Figure 1.42 Tile Horizontally stacks document windows one above another.

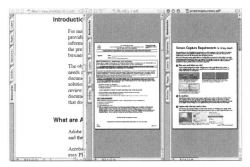

Figure 1.43 Tile Vertically displays documents side by side.

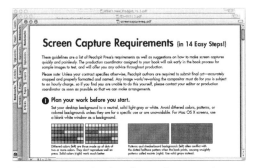

Figure 1.44 Cascade piles all open documents in a stack, with the active document on top.

Arranging Multiple Windows

Your computer screen can get quite messy when you have several PDF document windows open at once. Fortunately, Adobe Reader offers built-in functions that "tidy up" your document windows automatically.

To display all open documents:

◆ Choose either Window > Tile > Horizontally (Ctrl+Shift+K/Command+Shift+K) or Window > Tile > Vertically (Ctrl+Shift+L/Command+Shift+L).

Horizontal tiling displays open documents in a stack of horizontal windows (**Figure 1.42**).

Vertical tiling displays open documents next to each other in vertical windows (**Figure 1.43**).

To bring the active window to the front:

◆ Choose Cascade from the Window menu (Ctrl+Shift+J/Command+Shift+J).

The active (selected) document appears at the front of the stack, full size. Behind it, the title bars of all other open documents are displayed in a cascade (**Figure 1.44**).

ARRANGING MULTIPLE WINDOWS

Navigating in a Document Page

To move up or down within a page:

◆ Press the up or down arrow key.

or

Click and drag the scroll bars along the right side and bottom of the Document pane.

To move a page around:

1. Select the Hand tool from the Basic toolbar (**Figure 1.45**).

   The cursor changes to a little hand.

2. Click and drag a document page to reposition it.

   Release the mouse button, and the page will stay at the new position.

✔ Tip

■ While using any other Reader tool, if you want to switch to the Hand tool temporarily, hold down the spacebar. When you're through dragging your page around, release the spacebar to switch back to the tool you were using previously.

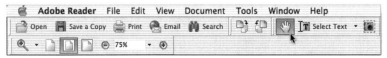

Figure 1.45 Click the little hand to grab your document and move it around.

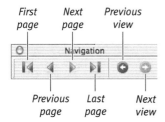

Figure 1.46 You'll find handy navigation buttons in the Navigation toolbar.

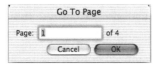

Figure 1.47 The Go to Page dialog box lets you jump instantly to any page.

Moving Between Document Pages

To go to the next page:

◆ Press the Page Down or right arrow key.

or

Click the Next Page button in either the Navigation toolbar (**Figure 1.46**) or the status bar.

To go to the previous page:

◆ Press the Page Up or left arrow key.

or

Click the Previous Page button in either the Navigation toolbar or the status bar.

To go to a specific page:

1. Choose View > Go To > Page (Ctrl+N/Command-N). The Go to Page dialog box appears (**Figure 1.47**).

2. Enter the number of the page you'd like to go to and click OK.

✔ Tip

■ You can also type a page number in the Current Page box on the status bar and press Enter/Return to jump to that page.

To go to the first page:

◆ Press Home on your keyboard.

or

Click the First Page button in either the Navigation toolbar or the status bar.

To go to the last page:

◆ Press End on your keyboard.

or

Click the Last Page button in either the Navigation toolbar or the status bar.

MOVING BETWEEN DOCUMENT PAGES

Printing a PDF Document

You can print a PDF file from Adobe Reader just as you would any other document.

To set up printing:

1. Choose File > Print Setup/Page Setup. This opens the Print Setup dialog box (**Figure 1.48**).

2. If necessary, change any of the page properties such as portrait or landscape orientation, paper size (choose from a list of pop-up sizes), or scale size for the document.

3. Click OK to save your choices and close the dialog box.

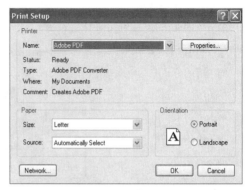

Figure 1.48 In the Print Setup/Page Setup dialog box, you can set some general printing options.

Printing Options

Most of the options in the Print dialog box can be left as they are by default. However, it's useful to know about a few of the options.

- The default choice under the Print What drop-down menu is to print just the document. You can also choose to print the document and the comments.

- The Page Scaling menu is set to Shrink Large Pages by default. If you're printing a large document, you may choose one of the other options, Fit to Paper, or None, instead. See the effect of your choice in the Preview area before you print.

- *Mac only:* If you're printing multiple copies of a document, you may click the Collated check box to have the copies collated, but be aware that the printing process will be greatly slowed down.

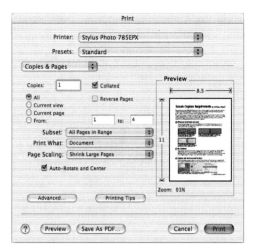

Figure 1.49 The Print dialog box lets you choose a number of printing options specifically for the current document.

To print a document from Adobe Reader:

1. Choose Print from the File menu (Ctrl+P/ Command+P) or click the Print button in the File toolbar. The Print dialog box appears (**Figure 1.49**).

2. For multiple copies, type the number of copies you want in the Print dialog box (**Figure 1.50**).

3. If you don't want to print the entire document, enter the starting and ending page numbers of the range to print.

4. Click OK/Print to send the document to the printer.

✔ Tip

■ Depending on your specific printer driver and operating system, your Print dialog box may look different from those shown here, but most of the same options should be available.

Figure 1.50 You can preview your document in the Print dialog box.

ADOBE
READER IN DEPTH

Now that you've mastered the basics of Adobe Reader, it's time to move on to some of the more advanced features that make Reader such a wonderful tool for viewing documents.

Often you'll want to go beyond simple document navigation and viewing, to such things as searching a document for a text string, copying text or an image, or changing the many Preference options that Reader provides, like displaying pages differently, having it read text aloud, and including multimedia in documents.

This chapter takes you on a tour of Adobe Reader's nitty-gritty details, so you can make this amazing software work for you!

Looking at Document Properties

Each PDF document has certain information associated with it; this data is known by the umbrella term Document Properties. It may tell you when the document was created, what application created it, or when it was last modified.

Adobe Reader groups Document Properties into four classes: Advanced, Description, Fonts, and Security.

The Description window contains information pertaining to the origin of a PDF file—details like its title and date of creation, the software used to create the original document, and file size and number of pages.

The Advanced options are Base URL, Search Index, Trapped, Binding, and Language. This information is of use to people creating professional documents in Acrobat. Security shows the security options that were set for the PDF file, such as requiring a password to alter the document, and whether you can print it, copy its content, add comments, fill in form fields, or sign the document.

To read the Document Properties for the current document:

1. Choose File > Document Properties (Ctrl+D/Command+D).

   or

   Choose Document Properties from the Document pane menu (**Figure 2.1**).

   The Document Properties dialog box appears (**Figure 2.2**).

2. Click a topic name to see the details in the right side of the window.

3. To close the Document Properties dialog box, click OK or Cancel.

Figure 2.1 Choose Document Properties from the Document pane menu.

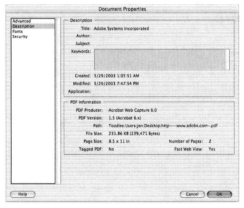

Figure 2.2 The Document Properties dialog box displays information about the currently active document.

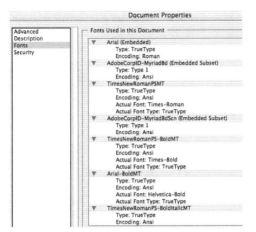

Figure 2.3 You can see a list of all the base fonts used in a PDF document.

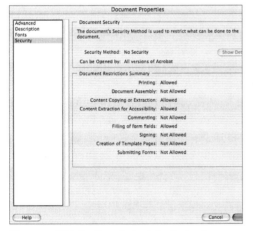

Figure 2.4 Click the Security topic to display the security options for the currently active document.

Checking fonts

The Fonts property lists all of the fonts in the document. You might want to check the fonts in a document to see if they are embedded in the PDF file; if they aren't embedded, Acrobat will substitute a similar font, which may or may not be acceptable in the final document. Note that in **Figure 2.3**, in several cases the font displayed on the screen in the PDF file is different from the actual font specified in the original design. (*e.g.,* Helvetica-Bold is represented on-screen by Arial-BoldMT.)

To see the fonts used in a PDF document:

◆ Choose File > Document Properties > Fonts (Ctrl+Alt+F/Command+Option+F), or choose Document Fonts from the Document pane menu.

A list of all fonts used in the document up to this point appears in the Fonts Used in this Document window.

Checking security

Many of the Document Security properties only matter to users of the full Acrobat Standard program. However, Adobe Reader users should still learn about them, especially those that define what users can do with the document.

To check document security:

◆ Choose File > Document Properties. In the Document Properties window, click the Security category on the left side. Security information for the document will appear on the right side of the window (**Figure 2.4**).

Reader Preferences

You can change a multitude of preferences in Adobe Reader that affect the way you view and navigate through documents. Although the default preferences work fine for most users, you may want to make some changes. Most of these options can be modified in the Preferences dialog box.

◆ **Accessibility (Figure 2.5)** lets you change the colors Adobe Reader uses to display documents, so that people with vision limitations can read them more easily.

◆ **Digital Signatures** allows you to change the look of the signature, enter a security method, and set validation options.

◆ **Forms** settings determine whether forms can calculate field values automatically, and other options affecting the look of forms.

◆ **Full Screen** lets you customize Full Screen mode, when all Reader controls and tools are hidden. The Navigation options determine how you navigate between pages and quit Full Screen mode. The Appearance options let you set the transition styles, background color, and so on.

READER PREFERENCES

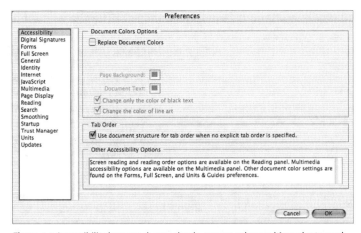

Figure 2.5 Accessibility lets you change the document colors so it's easier to read.

- **General** preferences allow you to set miscellaneous options relating to the user interface, such as how many recently viewed documents are listed, how to label tools and buttons, and how to open other document windows.

- **Identity** allows you to set the Reader user's ID, which is used with digital signatures.

- **Internet** lets you set the Web browser options and Internet options like connection speed.

- **JavaScript** allows you to enable Acrobat JavaScript.

- **Multimedia** lets you set the preferred media player and certain accessibility options like displaying subtitles and captions with certain types of multimedia.

- **Page Display** determines how PDF files are displayed onscreen.

- **Reading** includes the Read Out Loud options for volume, voice, speech attributes, reading order, and screen reader options.

- **Search** lets you set options for searching methods, including Fast Find.

- **Smoothing** allows you to set smoothing (antialiasing) options for text, line art, and images.

- **Startup** is where you set how documents are opened and how the Reader application opens.

- **Trust Manager** holds the settings for trusted, or secure, documents.

- **Units** lets you choose whether page measurements are shown in inches, picas, points, centimeters, or millimeters.

- **Update** sets Adobe Reader to check Adobe's Web site periodically for software updates.

READER PREFERENCES

To change Reader preferences:

1. Choose Edit > Preferences (Windows) or Adobe Reader > Preferences (Macintosh), or press Ctrl+K/Command+K.

2. In the left-hand list in the Preferences dialog box, click the topic whose preferences you want to set (**Figure 2.6**).

3. Select options and settings in the topic window on the right.

4. Click OK to save your changes or Cancel to close without saving.

✔ Tip

■ Keep in mind that changes made to Adobe Reader's preferences affect the way you'll view and work with all future documents within Reader. These changes aren't tied to specific documents.

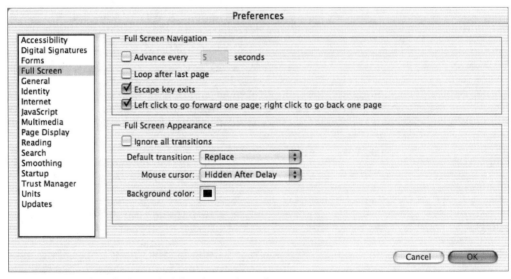

Figure 2.6 Choose from the list on the left to change the preferences.

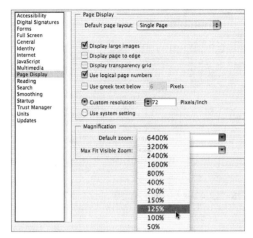

Figure 2.7 Use the Page Display preferences to can change the default magnification.

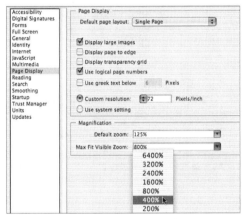

Figure 2.8 Also in the Page Display preferences you can change the maximum magnification by choosing a preset value or entering your own.

✔ Tip

■ The Fit Visible option, in which the width of the page fills the document window, is great for focusing on the content within a page rather than all the white space around that content.

Setting Magnification Preferences

Adobe Reader displays PDF files at a default magnification, which may not be the best one for your monitor. Fortunately, you can change this setting within Reader's preferences.

To change the default magnification:

1. Open the Preferences dialog box.

2. Choose Page Display from the list on the left.

3. Select a new default magnification level from the Default Zoom pop-up menu in the Magnification area (**Figure 2.7**), or type a new percentage in the text box.

4. Click OK. All documents will be displayed at the new default magnification.

If you've ever seen Reader zoom in too far when you change pages in Fit Visible mode, you'll appreciate Adobe Reader's ability to restrict Fit Visible's maximum zoom level.

To change the maximum magnification:

1. Open the Preferences dialog box.

2. Choose Page Display from the list on the left.

3. Select a new default magnification percentage from the Max Fit Visible Zoom pop-up menu in the Magnification area (**Figure 2.8**), or type a new value in the text box.

4. Click OK.

Reading Out Loud

Part of Adobe's efforts to accommodate visually impaired users, the Read Out Loud command will read a page or a whole document out loud. Choose from a variety of voices under the Reading preferences. To access the Reading preferences, open the Preferences dialog box, then choose Reading from the list of topics on the left. This will show the Read Out Loud Options (**Figure 2.9**). Choose a voice, pitch, and words per minute. You can also set the reading order and screen reader options.

To have a PDF file read out loud:

1. Choose View > Read Out Loud > and either Read This Page Only or Read to End of Document (**Figure 2.10**). You can also press Ctrl+Shift+V/Command+Shift+V for the current page or Ctrl+Shift+B/Command+Shift+B for the end of document.

   The voice will start reading.

2. To pause the reading, choose View > Read Out Loud > Stop or Pause.
   The reading will pause.

   You can also press Ctrl+Shift+C/Command+Shift+C to pause; press it again to continue reading.

3. To stop the reading, choose View > Read Out Loud > Stop or Pause, or press Ctrl+Shift+E/Command+Shift+E.

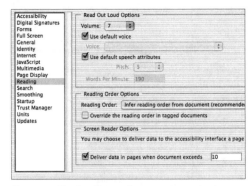

Figure 2.9 The Reading preferences determine how a document sounds when read out loud.

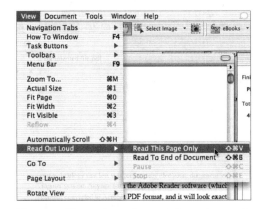

Figure 2.10 You can have all or part of your document read to you.

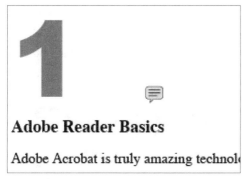

Figure 2.11 The note looks like a little yellow speech bubble.

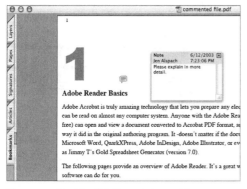

Figure 2.12 Double-click the note to read it.

Reading Notes

With Acrobat Standard or Professional, a user can add comments to a PDF document. Comments can be simple text notes, but they can also be file attachments, sound files, or even movie clips. Notes are probably the most common annotations.

To read Acrobat notes in Reader:

1. Locate the note that you wish to read on a PDF document. They look like tiny speech bubbles (**Figure 2.11**).

   Other types of annotations will display different icons, such as a rubber-stamp picture, a microphone, highlighted text, and so on.

2. Double-click the note (or other icon) with the Hand tool to display all of its text (**Figure 2.12**), as well as when and by whom it was written.

3. To close an expanded note, click the close box located in its upper-right corner. The note will collapse back to an icon.

✔ Tip

- In Adobe Reader you can click a note once to select it and drag it around a page, but you cannot otherwise alter or delete it. And because Reader doesn't allow you to save changes to a PDF document, the note will reappear in its original position the next time you open the document in Reader.

READING NOTES

Selecting Text and Images

Suppose you receive a PDF with wonderful content that you'd love to reuse in some other application. Depending on the security options set, Reader lets you copy text or images, edit an image in the program it was created in, or order prints of the images (once you've gotten permission from the document's creator, of course). However, before you can do anything with text or graphics in a PDF document, you first need to know how to select them. Adobe Reader offers two tools for selecting text and one for selecting images.

To select text using the Text Select tool:

1. Choose the Select Text tool in the Basic Tools toolbar (**Figure 2.13**).

2. Click and drag over the text you want to select (**Figure 2.14**). Note that the Select Text tool lets you select entire words, or just parts of words.

   After selecting, you can copy the text to the Clipboard and use it in another document. Note that the copied text is editable.

There's a trick to using the Select Text tool: If your selection extends any distance vertically, you may end up selecting parts of the page you don't want. For example, say you want to select part of one column in a table. As you drag downward, you end up selecting everything on the same row as your target text (**Figure 2.15**). To avoid this, press Ctrl/Command while selecting the text, and only text within your specified area will be selected.

Figure 2.13 Click the Select Text tool in the Basic toolbar.

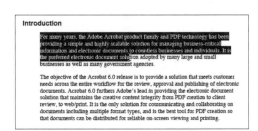

Figure 2.14 Drag the Select Text tool across the text you want to select.

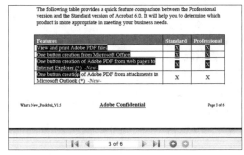

Figure 2.15 Dragging downward in a table selects rows, not columns.

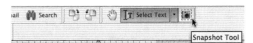

Figure 2.16 Click the Snapshot tool to the right of the Select Text tool.

Figure 2.17 Using the Snapshot tool, drag a rectangle around the area of the page you want to select.

Figure 2.18 The dialog box lets you know that the text was copied to the Clipboard.

Reader provides a second text-selection tool. Use the Snapshot tool to copy the contents of a table and all of its formatting to the Clipboard, so you can then paste it into another document or application. An important point to note is that the Snapshot tool converts the area you have selected to an image. The result may be pasted *as an image* into any application you wish, but the text and table data will not be editable.

To select text using the Snapshot tool:

1. Choose the Snapshot tool from the Basic Tools toolbar (**Figure 2.16**).

2. Click and drag diagonally across the document, drawing a rectangle around the text you wish to select (**Figure 2.17**). This brings up a dialog box telling you the text was copied to the Clipboard (**Figure 2.18**).

To select all text on a page:

◆ Choose Edit > Select All (Ctrl+A/ Command+A).

If the document is displayed in Single-Page made, all the text on the currently viewed page is selected. If the document is displayed in Continuous or Continuous-Facing mode, the Select All command selects the entire document.

✔ Tip

■ Remember, you can only select and copy text from a document if its creator has allowed this privilege in the Security options. See page 27 for more information on security.

SELECTING TEXT AND IMAGES

The Select Image tool lets you click on any image and copy it, exactly analogous to the Select Text tool. If you click on an image, the Select Image tool selects the entire image, as you would expect. If you click and drag within in an image, the tool will select and copy only the area within the rectangular area.

To select images:

1. Choose Select Image in the Basic Tools toolbar; it may be hidden under the Select Text tool (**Figure 2.19**).

2. Click and drag the Select Image tool over the area that you would like to select (**Figure 2.20**).

    A dashed-line rectangle will appear around the selected area as you drag. When you release the mouse button, the selected area shows the image reversed (**Figure 2.21**).

3. To deselect all selected text or images choose Edit > Deselect All (Ctrl+Shift+A/ Command+Shift+A) or just click somewhere else on the screen.

To copy selected text or images:

◆   With either text or graphics selected, choose Edit > Copy (Ctrl+C/ Command+C).

    The text or graphics selection will be copied to the Clipboard and is then available for pasting into another application.

✔ Tip

■   To make sure you've actually copied the right material, you can check the contents of the Clipboard. In Windows choose Window > Show Clipboard, in Mac go to the Finder and choose Edit > Show Clipboard.

Figure 2.19 The Select Image tool normally hides under the Select Text tool.

Figure 2.20 Using the Select Image tool, drag a rectangle around the graphic you want to select. A dashed-line border appears.

Figure 2.21 The image becomes reversed so you can see what was selected.

SELECTING TEXT AND IMAGES

Picture Tasks

Figure 2.22 The new Picture Tasks tools let you do some pretty cool things.

Figure 2.23 In addition to exporting and printing images, the Picture Tasks let you order prints online.

Figure 2.24 Adobe Reader will show you a note about the new Picture Tasks features.

A pretty cool new feature of Reader and Acrobat Standard 6.0 is the new Picture Tasks toolset that becomes available in the Tasks toolbar when you open a picture that was created in an Adobe application (JPEG format only) (**Figure 2.22**). Click the downward area next to Picture Tasks for a whole menu of commands (**Figure 2.23**).

■ **Export Pictures** from your PDF file and save them on your computer.

■ **Export and Edit Pictures** in Photoshop or Photoshop Elements, then save them on your computer.

■ **Print Pictures** to your printer from Reader.

■ **Order Prints Online** from a photo finisher and get them mailed to your house.

■ **Order Project Online** a whole PDF project, like a calendar or an album of photographs, created from either a Photoshop Elements or Photoshop Album template.

■ **How To Picture Tasks** take you through each of the above tasks step by step.

✔ Tip

■ When you open a file that contains an image, Reader and Acrobat will display a note telling about the new features (**Figure 2.24**).

Using the Search Command

Sometimes you need to locate a particular word or phrase within a document. Instead of trying to find it yourself by reading every page, you can get Adobe Reader to do the work for you using the Search command.

To search for a word or phrase:

1. Choose Edit > Search (Ctrl+F/ Command+F), or click the Search button in the File toolbar (**Figure 2.25**).

2. In the text field of the Search PDF pane, type the word or phrase you're looking for (**Figure 2.26**).

3. Choose what documents to search and exactly what Reader should be looking for.

4. Click Search. The first occurrence of the word or phrase will be highlighted.

5. Choose Edit > Search Results > Next Result (Ctrl+G/Command+G) to locate each successive instance of the word or phrase (**Figure 2.27**) or press Ctrl+Shift+G/Command+Shift+G to search for the previous result.

6. Once you've found what you're looking for, click Done at the bottom of the pane or Hide at the top to close the Search PDF pane.

✔ Tips

■ The various search options make it possible to search almost anywhere for a particular word or phrase. Internet searches are performed by Google. Note that searching the PDF files on your disk or the Internet can take a *very* long time.

■ If the term stands alone, then select the Whole Words Only check box. Otherwise, searching for "dog" will find "doggedness," "dog-eared," and "doggerel," as well as just plain "dog."

Figure 2.25 Press Ctrl+F/Command+F to access the Search options.

Figure 2.26 Enter the word or phrase you're looking for and any other options necessary.

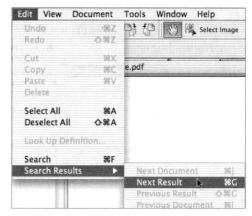

Figure 2.27 You can search again for the same word by pressing Ctrl+G/Command+G.

USING THE SEARCH COMMAND

ACROBAT eBOOK READER

3

In the latest release of Adobe Reader, Adobe combined eBook Reader with Adobe Reader as one application. Adobe's eBook Reader enables you to read eBooks—PDF files saved in a special format—on your computer: It's just like reading and turning the pages of a printed book. With eBook Reader you get the rich text and pictures of a PDF document, but without the complicated interface of Adobe Reader.

The eBook Reader does its best to make you think you're reading a traditional printed book. You can make annotations in your electronic book, add bookmarks at significant passages, and quickly flip to any page. But eBook Reader also includes up-to-date electronic features like searchable text, a built-in dictionary, and a built-in mechanism for downloading additional books. In addition, some eBooks include a license, provided by the seller, that allows you to lend and give your titles to other eBook Reader users, just as you might lend out your favorite paperback novel.

Activating Your eBook Reader Account

Adobe makes it nearly effortless to activate an account for eBooks. Before you start, make sure you're connected to the Internet so you can access the files you'll need from Adobe's Web site.

To activate your eBook Reader account:

1. Choose Tools > eBook Web Services > Adobe DRM Activator (**Figure 3.1**). This takes you to the Adobe DRM Activator Web site (**Figure 3.2**).

   DRM stands for Digital Rights Management.

2. If you already have an Adobe or Microsoft Net ID, enter it and the password. If not, you must create an Adobe ID.

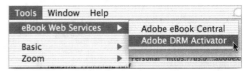

Figure 3.1 To activate eBooks, you need to visit the Adobe DRM Activator Web site.

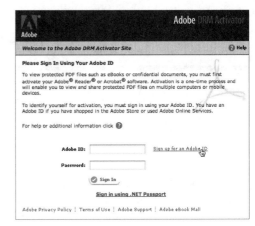

Figure 3.2 To activate eBooks, you'll need to set up an Adobe ID account.

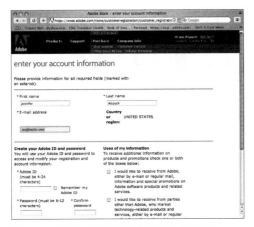

Figure 3.3 Once your account is set up, you can activate eBooks.

Figure 3.4 You can access eBooks Central from Reader to buy or download free eBooks.

3. To create an Adobe ID, click the "Sign up for an Adobe ID" link. This will take you to a page where you can set up your ID and profile (**Figure 3.3**).

Once you are signed in, you'll be at the Adobe Store Web site.

4. Go back to Reader and choose Tools > eBook Web Services > Adobe eBook Central.

This takes you to Adobe's Web site for eBooks, eBooks Central (**Figure 3.4**), where you can buy, sell, and lend books online.

✔ Tip

■ When you create your ID and profile you can update older eBooks to the new eBook format.

Downloading eBooks

At eBooks Central, you can choose to publish, sell, or "Read and enjoy" electronic books (**Figure 3.5**). Click the "Read and enjoy" link to go to the Adobe eBook Mall (**Figure 3.6**), where you can browse, buy eBooks from various retailers, or try out a book for three days from the Adobe eBook demonstration library. If you're looking for a specific book, take advantage of the Full Search feature on the Adobe eBook site, or browse by the genres literature and fiction, mystery and thrillers, and science fiction. All books on the Adobe eBook site are free for the downloading.

To search on Adobe's eBook site:

1. In Adobe Reader, choose File > My Bookshelf. This opens the My Bookshelf window (**Figure 3.7**).

2. At the top of the window, click the eBooks Online button. Your Web browser will open, showing the eBook Mall.

Figure 3.5 At eBooks Central, you'll find links to eBook retailers, a trial library, and free books from Adobe.

Figure 3.6 Adobe's eBook mall has a selection of free books in a variety of genres.

eBooks Online

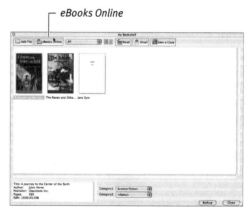

Figure 3.7 The My Bookshelf window in Reader shows the books you've downloaded.

3. Click the "Adobe eBook site" link under the General eBookstores heading (**Figure 3.8**). This opens Adobe's eBook site.

4. Click Full Search on the left (**Figure 3.9**).

5. Enter the title of the book or the author's name in the search fields, then click the Full Search button (**Figure 3.10**).

6. The results page shows all eBooks matching your search criteria (**Figure 3.11**).

Figure 3.8 Click the link to go to Adobe's eBook site.

Full Search

Figure 3.9 The Full Search button will help you find the book you're looking for.

Figure 3.10 Enter the information you know, and the Full Search button will do its best.

Figure 3.11 Here are the results of the search.

To download a free eBook:

1. In Adobe Reader, choose File > My Bookshelf. This opens the My Bookshelf window.

2. Click the eBooks Online button to access the eBook Mall.

3. Click the "Adobe eBook site" link in the General eBookstores area.

4. Choose a genre (literature and fiction, mystery and thrillers, or science fiction) in the Browse area on the left (**Figure 3.12**). The book choices for that genre appear (**Figure 3.13**).

5. Click a book title to see information about the book, including its price (free!) and a brief synopsis (**Figure 3.14**).

eBook genres

Figure 3.12 Click the browsing genres on the left to narrow your choices.

Figure 3.13 You'll see only books available in your chosen genre.

Figure 3.14 Before you make up your mind, you can get more information about the book.

Figure 3.15 Click the button to begin downloading your new book.

6. Click the Add to Order button to go to the download page.

7. On the download page, click the Click Here to Download Your eBook button (**Figure 3.15**) and the book will automatically download into the My Bookshelf window in Adobe Reader. You'll see a progress window as it downloads (**Figure 3.16**), and once it's done, a message letting you know that you can now read your eBook (**Figure 3.17**).

Figure 3.16 The progress window shows how much longer you have to wait.

Figure 3.17 You may now peruse it at your leisure.

Borrowing eBooks

You can borrow eBooks with Adobe Reader 6.0 just as you do from your neighborhood library. When you borrow an eBook from a library, it shows up in the My Bookshelf window with a timer icon. When your time is up, the book automatically disappears from the window.

To borrow an eBook from Adobe's library:

1. Open My Bookshelf and click the eBooks Online button.

   Your browser opens to the Adobe eBook Mall.

2. Click the Adobe eBook Library Demo link under the General eBookstores heading (**Figure 3.18**).

   The Adobe eBook Library window opens.

3. From the list on the left, choose a genre, then look for a book you'd like to borrow.

4. Click the title of the book you'd like to borrow.

5. In the Checkout window, choose how long you'd like to borrow the book and click Add to Bookbag (**Figure 3.19**).

6. Click the link to download the eBook you selected from the library (**Figure 3.20**). The eBook is downloaded to the My Bookshelf window in Adobe Reader.

Once your time is up, the book will disappear—in other words, it's been returned to the library.

Figure 3.18 Adobe's eBook Library Demo gives you a taste of online borrowing.

Figure 3.19 Add the book to your bookbag after you decide how long you want to keep it.

Figure 3.20 Click to leave the library with your borrowed book.

Figure 3.21 Click the eBooks Online button to shop for more eBooks.

Figure 3.22 You'll start at Adobe's eBook Mall Web site, a hub for eBook stores.

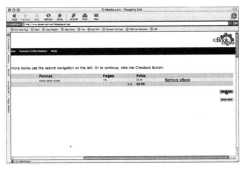

Figure 3.23 Most vendors let you choose more books before you pay for a purchase.

Purchasing and Organizing eBooks

Currently, a few online booksellers, including Barnes & Noble, Amazon.com, and Adobe itself, are offering a selection of free titles for trial use with Adobe Reader, with more available for purchase. Once you've downloaded a few titles, you can organize them into categories and, if the publisher gives permission, lend or give them away to other Reader users.

To download eBook titles for Reader:

1. Choose File > My Bookshelf. The My Bookshelf Dialog box appears.

2. Click the eBooks Online button (**Figure 3.21**).

3. When the eBook Mall page opens (**Figure 3.22**), select the vendor from which you want to download an eBook from among the General eBookstores, Educational eBookstores, and International eBookstores.

   or

   Enter "eBooks" in any search engine to find a vendor.

4. Navigate through the site to find a book. Choose a genre, then select your book by clicking on the title.

5. Choose the format option (Palm Reader, Microsoft Reader, or Adobe eBook Reader). When you've found a book you want to buy, make sure it's available in the Adobe Reader format (**Figure 3.23**).

(continues on next page)

PURCHASING AND ORGANIZING EBOOKS

6. To purchase the book, click the Buy button.

Once your order is processed, you can download the eBook (**Figure 3.24**) directly into your Adobe Reader bookshelf.

✔ Tips

■ Different vendors have different purchasing methods, so be sure to read and follow the purchasing instructions carefully.

■ It's usually a good idea to register with the eBook vendor, even if it's not an actual requirement.

Organizing your library

Over time, you may accumulate a lot of eBooks in your bookshelf. You may find yourself scrolling through screen after screen of thumbnails, searching for a particular title. But never fear: Adobe Reader can help.

The toolbar at the top of the My Bookshelf window provides a pop-up menu (**Figure 3.25**) that lets you view your eBooks by category. The categories are assigned when you download an eBook. You can also add a second category to your books. That way if you have tons of books under the Fiction category, you can sub-categorize them as romance, mystery, horror, or whatever.

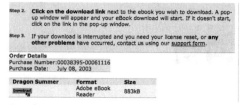

Figure 3.24 Your purchased book will download directly to your Reader bookshelf.

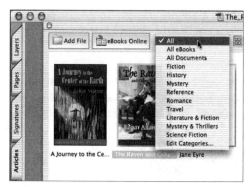

Figure 3.25 In the pop-up menu you can choose to see only one category of books.

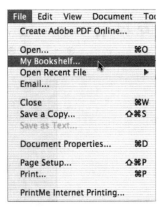

Figure 3.26 Choose My Bookshelf to open your bookshelf in Reader.

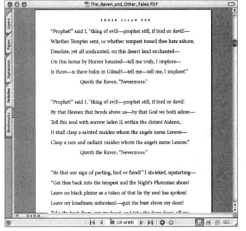

Figure 3.27 Click and type a new page number to go to a specific page.

Reading eBooks

Now that you have an eBook downloaded, you'll want to open it up and read it. Once you have a few books in your bookshelf, you'll be able to choose any book to read at your leisure. Adobe Reader's simple interface makes it easy to view eBooks.

To read an eBook:

1. Choose File > My Bookshelf (**Figure 3.26**). This opens the My Bookshelf window.

2. Click to select one of the eBooks you downloaded, then click the Read button.

   or

   Double-click a book in your bookshelf. The book opens to display the cover.

3. To turn the page, click the Next Page button in the status bar or press the down arrow on your keyboard.

4. To jump to a specific page, click in the Page Number field in the status bar and type in the page number (**Figure 3.27**).

   or

   Open the Pages pane to display thumbnails of all the book's pages. Click the thumbnail of whichever page you'd like to read.

   The page will be displayed in the reading area.

5. When you're finished reading an eBook, choose File > Close (Ctrl+W/Command+W) to close it, or choose File > My Bookshelf to pick another one.

(continues on next page)

READING EBOOKS

✔ Tips

- To enlarge or reduce an eBook's page size, click the Zoom In and Zoom Out buttons in the Zoom toolbar.

- Adobe Reader lets you change the look of the text to best suit your screen. In Preferences (Ctrl+K/Command+K) choose the Smoothing option on the left. Then check the Use CoolType check box to get better reading text (**Figure 3.28**).

- You can also have the program read an eBook aloud to you, although the electronic voice may not sound like your ideal narrator. Simply choose View > Read Out Loud. See Chapter 2 for more information on reading aloud.

- If you're using a laptop computer, you may want to rotate your eBook pages 90 degrees for more efficient use of your screen (**Figure 3.29**). Choose View > Rotate View > Counterclockwise. Holding your laptop sideways may not be the most comfortable position, but it's an option.

- The creators of individual eBooks may restrict users' ability to print or copy text or to lend or give the book to someone else. To check security permissions, choose File > Document Properties, then choose Security on the left.

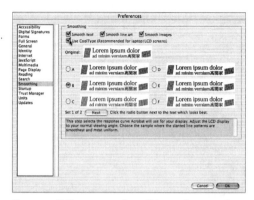

Figure 3.28 Change your Smoothing preferences for more readable type.

Figure 3.29 If you're using a laptop or lying down, you may want to rotate the pages.

Figure 3.30 Use the Commenting tools on your eBooks.

Figure 3.31 The Highlight tool lets you highlight sections of text.

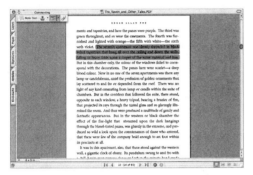

Figure 3.32 Click and drag the mouse across the text you want to highlight.

Commenting on an eBook

You can add various types of comments to your eBooks, just as you would for any PDF document. Add a note of thoughts on certain passages you've read, add a stamp, attach a file, or just highlight areas of text you want a friend to read.

To show the Commenting toolbar:

◆ Choose eBooks > Commenting Toolbar (**Figure 3.30**). The Commenting toolbar appears.

To highlight text:

1. Click the Highlight button in the Commenting toolbar (**Figure 3.31**) to begin highlighting.

2. Click the mouse button and drag across the passage you want to highlight (**Figure 3.32**).

3. Click the Highlight button again to stop using the highlighting tool.

The other commenting tools, like Underline and Strike Through, work just the same as Highlight.

✔ Tip

■ You can change the color and opacity of the highlighter and other commenting tools. For more on changing the properties of any of the editing tools, see Chapter 8.

COMMENTING ON AN EBOOK

To add notes:

1. Click the Note button in the Commenting toolbar (Ctrl+T/Command+T).
2. Click in the eBook where you want to create a note. A note window appears.
3. Type the text of your note in the window (**Figure 3.33**).

   When you're done, close the note window by clicking the close box. A speech bubble icon now marks the location of your collapsed note (**Figure 3.34**). Note that the comment's icon may not be a speech bubble; the appearance can be changed in the comment's properties.

✔ Tip

- Do you have more to say than will fit conveniently in a note? You can attach a file to the eBook, containing almost anything you like.

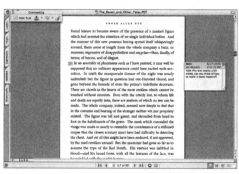

Figure 3.33 Enter your text in the note window.

EDGAR ALLAN POE

found leisure to become aware of the presence of a masked figure which had arrested the attention of no single individual before. And the rumour of this new presence having spread itself whisperingly around, there arose at length from the whole company a buzz, or murmur, expressive of disapprobation and surprise—then, finally, of terror, of horror, and of disgust.

In an assembly of phantasms such as I have painted, it may well be supposed that no ordinary appearance could have excited such sensation. In truth the masquerade licence of the night was nearly unlimited; but the figure in question had out-Heroded Herod, and gone beyond the bounds of even the prince's indefinite decorum.

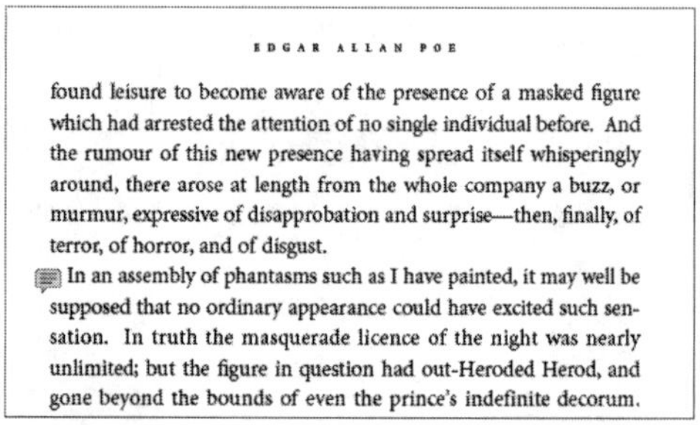

Figure 3.34 A speech bubble icon lets you know there's a note in the eBook.

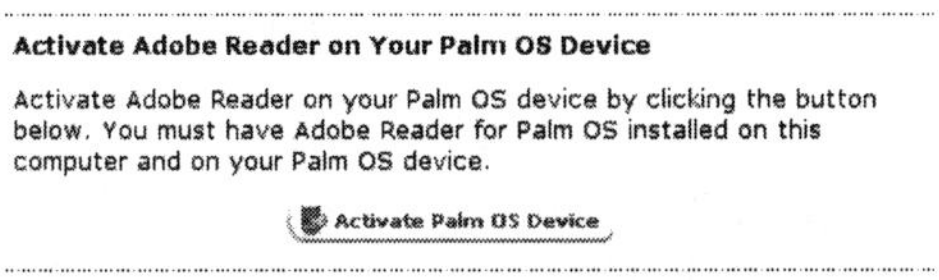

Figure 3.35 Click the Activate Palm OS Device button and begin reading your eBook on your Palm.

Using eBooks on Mobile Devices

With Adobe Reader 6, you can now download eBooks on a mobile device such as a Palm. Reader will even reflow the text in the space allowable by the Palm device. To use this feature, you must download and activate the eBook services with Adobe Reader 6 on both your Palm and the desktop, laptop, or tablet computer that you have synchronized with that Palm OS device.

To enable a Palm as an eBook reader:

1. Put the Palm OS device it its cradle, connected to the computer.

2. In Reader, choose Tools > eBook Web Services > Adobe DRM Activator.

   The Adobe eBook account activator site appears.

3. Enter your Adobe ID and password.

   See "To activate your eBook Reader account" earlier in the chapter for more information on activating your Adobe eBook account.

4. On the page that appears, click the Activate Palm OS Device button (**Figure 3.35**).

   Now you can read eBooks on your handheld as you would on your computer.

Sharing Your eBooks

One of the best things about reading a great new book is sharing your discovery with a friend. But if you're frustrated at lending books out and never seeing them again, you'll love Adobe Reader's sharing capabilities. If the publisher of the eBook has allowed this feature in the security permissions for the document, you can lend your eBooks out to as many friends as you'd like, and still keep a copy for yourself. You can even email the eBook for maximum convenience.

To email or lend eBooks:

1. Open My Bookshelf and click the thumbnail of the eBook you wish to email.

2. Click the Email button (**Figure 3.36**) to activate your default email program.

   The eBook file will automatically be attached to the email.

3. Fill in the various fields in the message, like the recipient's name and a subject line, and send the eBook (**Figure 3.37**).

Email button

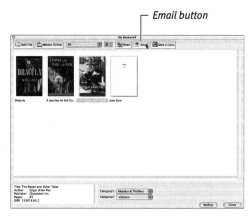

Figure 3.36 When you click the email button, your email program will launch so you can send an eBook.

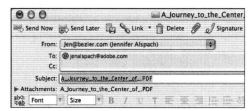

Figure 3.37 The eBook is already attached to the email, just tell it who to go to and send.

CREATING PDFS

To convert documents to Portable Document Format (PDF) in Acrobat, you need Acrobat Standard or Professional. You can create a PDF from a single file, multiple files, a Web page, or images from a scanner or the Clipboard. And if you need help, Acrobat 6's wonderful new How To feature can tell you, step by step, exactly how to create PDF files.

You also can create PDFs directly from within authoring applications. This saves you tons of time, since you can open the document directly in Acrobat 6 or Adobe Reader.

Converting a File to PDF

The first step in creating a PDF is to choose your method. You can create a PDF from a file, from multiple files, from a scanner, or from a Web page. Pick a creation method from the Create PDF submenu under the File menu (**Figure 4.1**). You can create a PDF from a variety of file types, including BMP, Compuserve GIF, HTML, JPEG, JPEG 2000, Microsoft Word, PCX, PNG, PostScript/EPS, Text file, and TIFF.

To create a PDF from a file:

1. Choose File > Create PDF > From File. This brings up the Open dialog box.

2. Navigate to the file, then click Open (**Figure 4.2**).

   The file will open in Acrobat 6.

3. Select File > Save as.

4. Enter a name for the PDF, and select a location where you want to save it. Press Enter or click Save.

   The .PDF extension is automatically added to your file name, and the new PDF is saved at the chosen location.

Figure 4.1 The Create PDF submenu has several options.

Figure 4.2 Choose the file you want to open as a PDF then click Open.

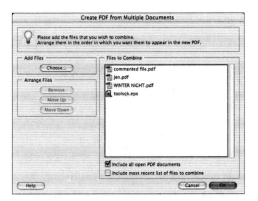

Figure 4.3 The Create PDF from Multiple Documents dialog box looks more complicated than it is.

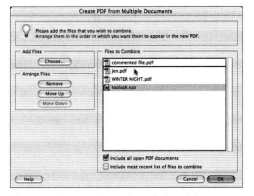

Figure 4.4 You can change the ordering of documents in your PDF or change your mind about adding a document.

To create a PDF from multiple files:

1. Choose File > Create PDF > From Multiple Files. This brings up the Create PDF from Multiple Documents dialog box (**Figure 4.3**).

2. Under the Add Files heading, click the Choose button to browse for files to add.

3. When the Open dialog box appears, choose a file and click the Add button. You can select multiple files at one time using the Shift and Control keys.

   Back in the Create PDF from Multiple Documents dialog box, the Files to Combine pane lists files that will appear in your new PDF. The file you just chose is added to the list.

4. Under the Arrange Files heading, use the Remove, Move Up, and Move Down buttons to change the order in which the files will be added to the PDF.

   You can also click and drag files into place (**Figure 4.4**).

5. Once you've added and arranged all of the files you want to combine, click OK. Acrobat will find all the files, and copy them into a new PDF file, temporarily named "binder1.pdf," until you save it with a new name.

CONVERTING A FILE TO PDF

To create a PDF from a scanner:

1. Place the document you want to convert to PDF in your scanner.

2. Choose File > Create PDF > From Scanner. This brings up the Create PDF from Scanner dialog box (**Figure 4.5**).

3. Choose your scanner from the Device pop-up menu.

4. Choose single- or double-sided from the Format pop-up menu.

5. Click the radio button for how you want the file to be saved—as a new PDF or added to the current document.

6. Select your compatibility and compression options, then click the Scan button.

   The new scanned file will open as a new PDF or be added to your open PDF, according to the Destination option you chose.

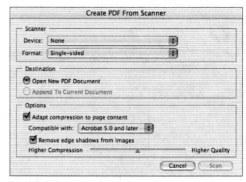

Figure 4.5 In the Create PDF from Scanner dialog box, you can change compression and compatibility settings.

Figure 4.6 Enter the URL of the Web site you want to open as a PDF.

Figure 4.7 Acrobat will warn you if the file will be large.

Creating PDFs from Web Pages

You can download a Web page or an entire Web site into Acrobat and convert it into a PDF document. If you first download only a single page or level of the site, and then want some of the linked pages, you can append more pages or levels later.

To create a PDF from a Web page:

1. Choose File > Create PDF > From Web Page (Shift+Ctrl+O/Shift+Command+O). The Create PDF from Web Page dialog box appears.

2. In the URL text field, enter the address of the Web site you want to make into a PDF (**Figure 4.6**).

3. Under the Settings heading, choose how many levels of this site you want Acrobat to download.

   If you click Get Entire Site, you may get a very large PDF document. Acrobat will warn you if that's the case (**Figure 4.7**).

(continues on next page)

CREATING PDFs FROM WEB PAGES

4. Click the Settings button in the Create PDF from Web Page dialog box to open the Web Page Conversion Settings (Windows) or Web Page Capture Settings (Mac) dialog box. Click the tabs to adjust the General (**Figure 4.8**) and Page Layout (**Figure 4.9**) settings, then click OK.

5. In the Create PDF from Web Page dialog box, click Create to download the Web page and open it as a new PDF file.

✔ Tip

■ You can also access previously saved Web pages on your computer. In the Create PDF from Web Page dialog box, click the Browse button to display any HTML files already saved on your hard drive.

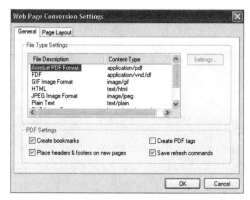

Figure 4.8 Adjust the General settings for your PDF.

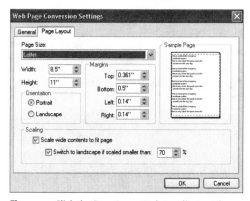

Figure 4.9 Click the Page Layout tab to adjust settings.

Web Page Conversion Settings

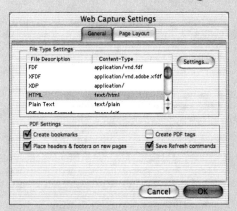

Figure 4.10 Click a file type in the list to adjust settings.

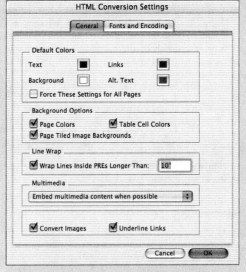

Figure 4.11 In the HTML Conversion Settings dialog box, you can determine how Acrobat handles Web page conversions.

The General and Page Layout settings accessed through the Create PDF from Web Page dialog box let you choose just how the files download. In the General tab, choose one of the file types and then click the Settings button to alter how Acrobat converts that specific file type.

For example, to change the download settings for an HTML page, click HTML in the File Type Settings list (**Figure 4.10**), then click the Settings button. This opens up the HTML Conversion Settings dialog box (**Figure 4.11**). Here you can set the colors for text and background colors and change how Acrobat handles backgrounds, tables, text wrapping, multimedia, links, and images. Once the settings are as you'd like them, click OK to go back to the Web Page Conversion Settings (Windows) or Web Page Capture Settings (Macintosh) dialog box.

Click the Page Layout tab if you want to set the page size, orientation, margins, and scaling. When you're satisfied with all the settings, click OK to go back to the Create PDF from Web Page dialog box.

While these options may be useful at some point, the defaults are pretty much what you would want to use in almost all cases.

When you download a Web page as a PDF, it may contain hyperlinks to other Web pages. When you put the mouse pointer over a link, the pointer turns into a small hand marked with a plus sign (**Figure 4.12**). This indicates that clicking the link will open the linked page as a PDF file in Acrobat.

To open a Web link:

1. In your active document, click a link.

   The Specify Weblink Behavior dialog box appears (**Figure 4.13**).

2. Choose whether you want to open the link in Acrobat or in your Web browser.

   If you switch to opening links in your Web browser, the pointer changes to a hand with a *W* on it (**Figure 4.14**).

3. To change this setting permanently, choose Edit > Preferences.

   The Preferences dialog box appears (**Figure 4.15**).

4. Choose Web Capture from the list on the left.

   The Web Capture settings appear.

5. Choose the desired option from the Open Web links pop-up menu.

Figure 4.12 The pointer turns into a hand with a plus sign when it's over a link.

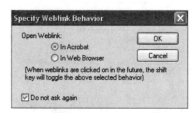

Figure 4.13 In the Specify Weblink Behavior dialog box, choose whether you want to the file to open in a browser or as a PDF.

Figure 4.14 If you switch the settings in the Specify Weblink Behavior to browser, the pointer turns into a hand with a W.

Figure 4.15 The Web Capture settings panel of the Preferences dialog box.

Figure 4.16 You can also convert a Web page from within Internet explorer.

Figure 4.17 You may have to tell Internet Explorer to show the PDF toolbar.

Creating PDFs in Other Applications

You can generate a PDF directly from within many authoring applications, without first saving the file as a PostScript file, as you had to in previous versions of Acrobat. Acrobat 6 provides several mechanisms for this purpose.

To create a PDF in Internet Explorer (Windows):

1. In Internet Explorer, go to the Web page you want to convert to a PDF.

2. Click the Convert Current Web page to PDF File button to open the Convert Web Page to Adobe PDF dialog box (**Figure 4.16**).

   If you have Windows XP and don't see the PDF icon, choose View > Toolbars > Adobe PDF (**Figure 4.17**).

3. In the Convert Web Page to Adobe PDF dialog box, enter a filename, choose a location, and click Save.

   Once you click the Save button, the Web page will save the Web page as a PDF in the location you chose, and open it in Acrobat 6.

To create a PDF with PDFMaker in Microsoft Office:

1. In the Microsoft Office application (Word, Excel, PowerPoint), open the file you want to convert. I use Microsoft Word for this example.

2. Choose Adobe PDF > Convert to Adobe PDF (**Figure 4.18**) or click Convert to Adobe PDF in the toolbar. This opens the Save Adobe PDF File As dialog box.

3. Enter a file name for the document, choose a destination, then click Save.

   The Acrobat PDFMaker progress window appears, displaying the progress on saving the file (**Figure 4.19**). The converted file will automatically open in Acrobat 6.

To create a PDF in Macintosh OS X:

1. In the Microsoft Office application (Word, Excel, PowerPoint), open the file you want to convert. I use Microsoft Word for this example.

2. Choose File > Print to open the Print dialog box (**Figure 4.20**).

3. Choose Adobe PDF from the Printer pop-up menu at the top of the dialog box.

4. Click the Save as PDF button to bring up the Save to File dialog box (**Figure 4.21**).

5. Enter a name for the file, choose a destination, then click Save to save the file as a PDF.

6. The file does not automatically open in Acrobat. If you want to open it, choose File > Open in Acrobat 6 and choose the file you saved.

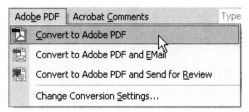

Figure 4.18 You can convert a file from within any Office application with this special menu.

Figure 4.19 The progress window shows you how much longer you'll have to wait.

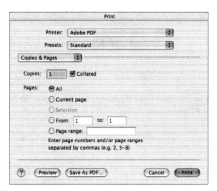

Figure 4.20 To convert a file to PDF from within Office on a Mac, you have to go through the Print dialog box.

Figure 4.21 Enter a name for the PDF and choose a location to save it in.

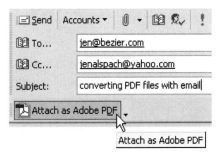

Figure 4.22 Microsoft Outlook also has a special button that creates PDFs.

Figure 4.23 Choose the file you want to send as a PDF.

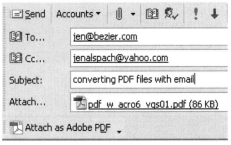

Figure 4.24 Your file is attached to the email and ready to send.

To create and email a PDF in Microsoft Outlook (Windows):

1. In Outlook, create your new email.

2. Click the Attach as Adobe PDF button (**Figure 4.22**) to attach your file and have it converted to a PDF so you can send it in an email.

   This brings up the Choose File to Attach as Adobe PDF dialog box.

3. Navigate to the file you want to send and click the Open button (**Figure 4.23**). This brings up the Save Adobe PDF File As dialog box.

4. Enter a name and save location, and click the Save button.

   This launches the application in which the file you're converting was created. Acrobat PDFMaker automatically processes the information and converts the file into a PDF. Once it's finished, you'll see the attached file in the Outlook email message (**Figure 4.24**).

To create a PDF from PowerPoint and send for review:

1. Open the presentation in PowerPoint.

2. Click the Convert to PDF and Send for Review button in the toolbar (**Figure 4.25**).

3. This brings up the Save Adobe PDF File As dialog box. Enter a name for the PDF file, choose a save location, then click the Save button (**Figure 4.26**). PDFMaker's progress bar will appear.

4. When the file is saved, the Send by Email for Review dialog box will appear, asking for your email address (**Figure 4.27**). Enter your email address and click OK.

5. The next dialog box allows you to enter destination information (**Figure 4.28**). Enter the recipient's email address, and any cc: or bcc: recipients. You can also change the subject and add to the explanatory message to reviewers.

6. Click the Send button to send the email.

Figure 4.25 You can choose to convert a file and send it for review in only a few steps.

Figure 4.26 Don't forget to pick a location for the saved file.

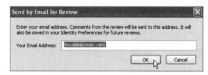

Figure 4.27 The Send by Email for Review dialog box will ask you for the email address from which you're sending.

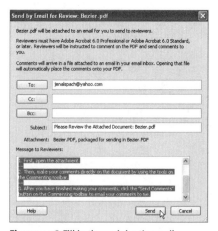

Figure 4.28 Fill in the recipient's email address, and you're ready to send.

WORKING WITH ACROBAT STANDARD

Working in Acrobat 6 Standard is very much like working in Adobe Reader. The user interface has the same basic elements, plus a few more that handle the enhanced capabilities of Acrobat. This chapter presumes that you're familiar with the basics of the Adobe Reader interface and points out only those things that are different in Acrobat. Refer to Chapters 1 and 2 if you need a refresher.

Acrobat lets you do more than just read a PDF file; you can also edit its text, add pages, add links, create navigational structures, and even turn a PDF into a multimedia presentation with dazzling transitions between pages. I'll deal with the more complex features in later chapters.

Starting and Quitting Acrobat

Starting Acrobat is no different from starting any other Windows or Mac program.

To run Acrobat:

◆ Locate the Acrobat icon and double-click it (**Figure 5.1**).

 While Acrobat is loading, the Acrobat screen appears (**Figure 5.2**), and the plug-ins that are in the Acrobat Plug-in folder also load.

To quit Acrobat:

◆ Choose Exit (Windows)/Quit (Mac) from the File/Acrobat menu (Ctrl+Q/ Command+Q).

 Any open documents close automatically. If changes were made in a document, a dialog box appears, asking whether you want to save those changes.

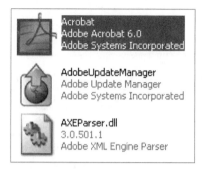

Figure 5.1 Double-click the Acrobat icon to run the program.

Figure 5.2 The Acrobat splash screen tells you what plug-ins are loading.

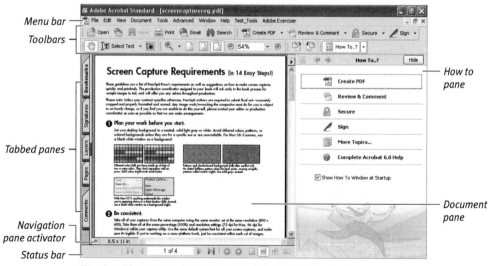

Figure 5.3 The main application screen of Acrobat 6.0 Standard.

Figure 5.4 The File toolbar holds tools for basic Acrobat functions.

Figure 5.5 The Tasks toolbar offers tools for marking up and commenting on documents.

Hand tool   Snapshot tool

Figure 5.6 Tools in the Basic toolbar are used for changing and adding to documents.

Understanding the Acrobat Screen

The Acrobat interface offers the same types of tools you're familiar with from Adobe Reader: menus, toolbars, and panes. The main difference is that you'll find more of them in Acrobat. The overall structure of the Acrobat and Reader windows is the same: Navigation pane on the left, Document pane on the right, and status bar along the bottom (**Figure 5.3**). New in Acrobat 6.0 Standard is the How To area on the right of the screen. If you don't require the help, click the Hide button in the upper-right corner to hide the How To program.

Acrobat's toolbars

Acrobat has all the same toolbars as Adobe Reader and two more: Commenting and Basic. Fortunately, toolbars work exactly the same way in both applications.

◆ The **File** toolbar (**Figure 5.4**) holds tools for opening, saving, and finding words within files, as well as tools that handle converting documents to PDF and emailing a document from within Acrobat.

◆ The **Tasks** toolbar (**Figure 5.5**) provides tools for creating PDFs, commenting on PDFs, PDF security, and signing PDFs.

◆ The tools in the **Basic** toolbar (**Figure 5.6**) allow you to change the contents of a PDF.

Acrobat's menus

Acrobat has the same assortment of menus as Adobe Reader, but there are more commands in each Acrobat menu.

- The **File** menu (**Figure 5.7**) handles basic file operations such as opening, closing, creating and printing PDFs, and setting document-specific parameters.

- The **Edit** menu (**Figure 5.8**) provides basic search tools and editing commands, including Copy, Cut, Paste, and Check Spelling.

- The **View** menu (**Figure 5.9**) allows you to adjust how Acrobat displays the document: its magnification and orientation, the number of pages shown at once, color space, and fonts. You can also show or hide panes and toolbars here.

Figure 5.7 Look in the File menu for commands to accomplish most basic Acrobat tasks.

Figure 5.8 In the Edit menu, you'll find the Acrobat preferences as well as commands that allow you to search for and alter content.

Figure 5.9 The View menu lets you fine-tune Acrobat's appearance.

UNDERSTANDING THE ACROBAT SCREEN

Figure 5.10 The Document menu holds commands for commenting on and signing documents.

Figure 5.11 The Tools menu lets you more serious stuff, like commenting and advanced editing.

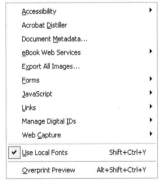

Figure 5.12 The Advanced menu gives you access to options like Accessibility, Acrobat Distiller, Java-Script, and links.

◆ The **Document** menu (**Figure 5.10**) allows you to comment on, attach files to, and digitally sign a PDF, and add headers, footers, watermarks, backgrounds, and pages. Use the tools here to add, import and export comments.

◆ The **Tools** menu (**Figure 5.11**) contains industrial-strength commands for operations such as commenting, processing, viewing, and editing.

◆ The **Advanced** menu (**Figure 5.12**) holds commands for using Acrobat Distiller, editing metadata, and exporting images, and the submenus Accessibility, eBook Web Services, Forms, JavaScript, Links, Digital IDs, and Web Capture.

(continues on next page)

UNDERSTANDING THE ACROBAT SCREEN

◆ The **Window** menu's commands (**Figure 5.13**) let you customize your workspace. You can choose not only which document window is in the foreground, but how Acrobat arranges multiple documents.

◆ In the **Help** menu (**Figure 5.14**) you'll find assistance, including access to Acrobat Help (itself a huge PDF) and Adobe's Web-based support. A new addition to the Help menu is the How To feature, which opens a special window to take you step by step through many types of task.

✔ Tip

■ The Window menu in the Mac OS doesn't contain the Clipboard Viewer command. Instead, go to the Finder and select Edit > Show Clipboard.

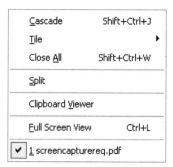

Figure 5.13 The Window menu allows you to specify how documents are shown in the workspace.

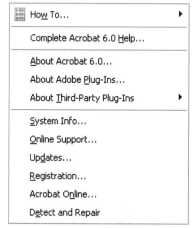

Figure 5.14 The Help menu gives you access to Adobe Acrobat's Help file and the How To section.

Figure 5.15 Click a bookmark in the Bookmarks pane to jump to its specified location.

Figure 5.16 The Signatures pane displays all signatures that have been appended to the document.

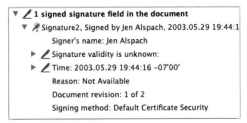

Figure 5.17 This window shows information about who has digitally signed the document and whether it has been altered since it was signed.

Figure 5.18 The Layers pane shows the name and status of layers in the document.

Figure 5.19 The Pages pane displays thumbnail views of each page in the document.

Acrobat's panes

Acrobat's panes work just like those in Adobe Reader. The Navigation pane contains the Bookmark, Signatures, Pages (formerly Thumbnails), and Layers panes, and the Comments pane, new in Acrobat 6. Extra commands in the pane menus allow you to edit their contents.

◆ The **Bookmarks** pane displays the bookmarks added to the PDF by the document's author (**Figure 5.15**). Click a bookmark to jump to that point in the document. You can create and edit bookmarks as well. For more information, see Chapter 6.

◆ The **Signatures** pane shows any digital signatures that have been added to the document (**Figure 5.16**). The pane also displays information about the digital signature (**Figure 5.17**). Learn more about digital signatures in Chapter 11.

◆ The **Layers** pane displays the layers that were transferred from the authoring application. You can examine a layer and show or hide its contents (**Figure 5.18**).

◆ The **Pages** pane displays a small image, or thumbnail, of each page of the document (**Figure 5.19**). You can move to a page quickly by clicking its thumbnail. You can add or delete pages, or change the order of pages in a document, just by dragging their thumbnails around. Thumbnails are discussed in more detail in Chapter 6.

(continues on next page)

UNDERSTANDING THE ACROBAT SCREEN

◆ The **Comments** pane displays a list of the comments and annotations that have been added to the document (**Figure 5.20**). For more information on comments, see Chapter 8.

Acrobat has several other panes as well, which you can access through the View > Navigation Tabs submenu.

◆ The **Articles** pane lists the articles defined by the document's author (**Figure 5.21**). Double-click an article to read it from the beginning. Articles are discussed in more detail in Chapter 6.

◆ The **Destinations** pane shows destinations (named link targets) that have been established in the document (**Figure 5.22**). Double-click a destination to jump to that spot in the document.

◆ The **Info** pane shows you the position of the mouse pointer relative to the top-left corner of the document (**Figure 5.23**). If you're making a selection (for example, selecting text or graphics or defining a form field), the pane also shows the dimensions of that selection. You can change the unit of measurement from the Info pane's menu: points, inches, or millimeters.

✔ Tip

■ Customizing the display and arrangement of panes works exactly the same way in Acrobat as it does in Adobe Reader (see Chapter 1).

Figure 5.20 The Comments pane displays all the comments appended to the document.

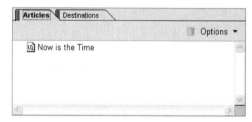

Figure 5.21 The Articles pane lists any articles defined in the document.

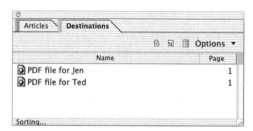

Figure 5.22 The Destinations pane shows links that have been set up between documents.

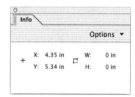

Figure 5.23 The Info pane shows you the position of the mouse pointer relative to the top-left corner of the document.

Figure 5.24 Choose the file you want to open and click Open.

Opening PDF Files

Opening and closing PDF files is pretty straightforward. You can open files whether Acrobat is running or not. As in most applications, there are a number of ways to open and close documents. This section covers my preferred methods.

To open a PDF file from within Acrobat:

◆ Choose Open from the File menu (Ctrl+O/ Command+O) to display the Open dialog box; then select the PDF you want to open and click the Open button (**Figure 5.24**). The file opens.

To open a PDF file outside Acrobat:

◆ Drag the PDF file you want to open onto the Acrobat icon.

or

Double-click the PDF's icon.

The file opens.

To close a PDF file:

◆ Choose Close from the File menu (Ctrl+W/ Command+W).

or

Click the close box in the document window.

The file closes. If you've made changes to the document, a dialog box will ask if you want to save the changes before closing the file.

Zooming

There are three basic ways to change the magnification of your document: using tools in the status bar, using the Zoom tools, and using the Dynamic Zoom tool. In the Zoom toolbar, you can choose a preset magnification, or use the magnifying glass to click in your document or select a rectangular area to view on the Acrobat page. You can also choose a magnification from the status bar and the View menu. Dynamic Zoom lets you use the mouse to zoom in or out.

To zoom using the status bar:

◆ Click on the pop-up menu beside the current magnification and choose a preset zoom amount, click the Zoom In or Zoom Out button, or click in the Zoom field and type in the amount (**Figure 5.25**).

To use the Zoom tools:

1. In the Zoom toolbar, click the tool you wish to use, either Zoom In (the "plus" magnifying glass) or Out (the "minus" magnifying glass) (**Figure 5.26**).

   If the Zoom toolbar isn't visible, choose Tools > Zoom > Zoom toolbar.

2. Click on the page to zoom in (or out) to the next preset amount.

3. If you want to zoom in on one section of the page, click and drag a marquee around that area on the page with the Zoom In tool.

To use the Dynamic Zoom tool:

1. In the Zoom toolbar, click the Dynamic Zoom tool (**Figure 5.27**).

2. Click on the page and drag up and to the left or right to zoom in. Drag down and to the left or right to zoom out.

Figure 5.25 Choose a preset magnification, type in your own zoom value, or click the zoom in or out buttons.

Figure 5.26 Click the Zoom In tool for a close-up and the Zoom Out tool for the big picture.

Figure 5.27 Click the Dynamic Zoom tool to control the magnification with your mouse.

ZOOMING

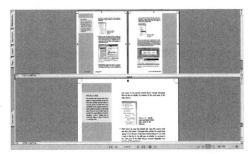

Figure 5.28 Split the window to see two different views of the same document.

Using Split Window View

The split view allows you to see two panes of the same document. It's useful for looking at pages later in the document without losing your place. You can also zoom in or navigate to a different page in one pane without affecting the other pane.

To split the view:

◆ Choose Window > Split.

The window automatically splits into two panes arranged one above the other (**Figure 5.28**). You can now change the page and view displayed in each of these panes without affecting the other pane. To go back to a single pane, choose Window > Split again.

Viewing Layers

You can now view layers in Acrobat files. The layers must be created in another application that works with layers and must be saved as an Acrobat 6.0 PDF file with compatibility of Acrobat 6.0. Open the file in Acrobat, and you can show and hide layers or examine the specific layers.

To view layers:

1. Click the Layers tab at the left of the Acrobat window.

   or

   Choose View > Navigation tabs > Layers.

   A list of the layers in the document will appear (**Figure 5.29**).

2. To hide a layer, click the eye to the left of that layer within the Layers pane.

3. Click again in the left column to make the eye, and the layer, reappear.

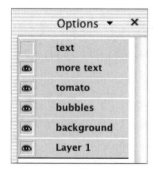

Figure 5.29 The list of layers in the document shows which of the layers are visible.

VIEWING LAYERS

Adding Headers and Footers

It's pretty easy to add headers and footers, including page numbers, all in Acrobat. Headers and footers take advantage of the document margins to add document information such as date, title, and page numbers.

The Headers and Footers Dialog Box

If you select Document > Add Headers & Footers, Acrobat presents you with the Add Headers & Footers dialog box (**Figure 5.30**). This dialog box is somewhat confusing at first, but with a bit of exploration it's quite easily usable.

Acrobat's headers and footers can contain three pieces of information: the current page number, the current date, and some arbitrary text that you supply. These pieces of information may be printed justified at the left or right margins of the page or centered.

(continues on next page)

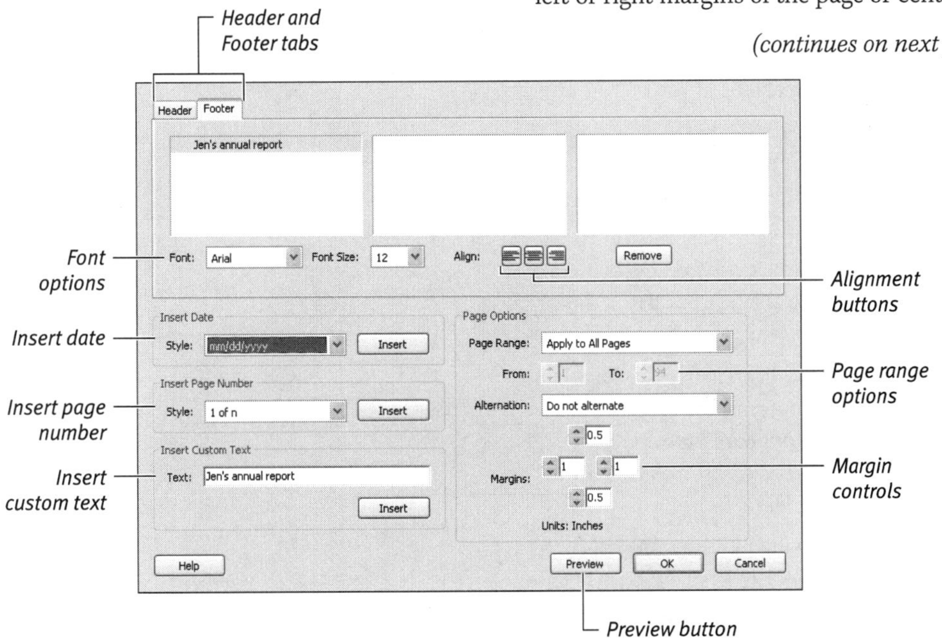

Header and Footer tabs

Font options
Insert date
Insert page number
Insert custom text
Alignment buttons
Page range options
Margin controls
Preview button

Figure 5.30 With so many settings, your header or footer can look just the way you want it to.

At the top of the dialog box are three boxes, specifying the information that should be printed at left-justified, centered, and right-justified positions within the header or footer. Below these are a series of menus that allow you to add the date, page number, or arbitrary text to each of these lists. To add, say, a page number to the centered list, click on the center box and then, in the Insert Date area, select a Style in the pop-up menu and click the Insert button. This will add the page number to the centered list.

To move an item to a different list (from centered to right justified, perhaps), select the item in its present list and click the appropriate Align icon (just below the three lists).

To add a header or footer:

1. Choose Document > Add Headers & Footers.

   This opens the Add Headers & Footers dialog box.

2. Click the Header or Footer tab at the top of the dialog box.

   The information is the same in both tabs, only the final placement of the text on the page is different.

3. Choose the font, size, and alignment options for your header or footer.

4. Click the appropriate Insert button to add a date, page number, and custom text (for example, a title). Set the style for your date and page numbering.

5. In the Page Options area, use the Page Range menu to determine whether your header or footer appears on every page, alternate pages, and so on. Select margin sizes for the header or footer.

6. When you're finished adding information, you can click the Preview button to see what it will look like (**Figure 5.31**).

7. Once your header or footer looks the way you want it to, click OK.

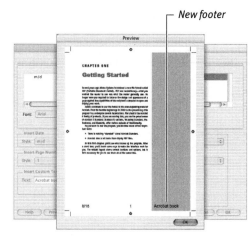

New footer

Figure 5.31 Click the Preview button to see how your document will look with the new header or footer before you accepting it.

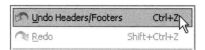

Figure 5.32 Choose Edit > Undo Headers/ Footers to remove a newly minted header or footer.

Figure 5.33 Select the custom text and click the Remove button to get rid of it.

To remove and restore a header or footer:

1. Choose Edit > Undo Headers/Footers (Ctrl+Z/Command+Z) to remove a header or footer you've just added (**Figure 5.32**).

   If you've made other changes to the document since you added the header or footer, you'll have to repeat the Edit > Undo command multiple times.

2. To restore a header or footer you've just removed, choose Edit > Redo Headers/Footers (Ctrl+Shift+Z/ Command+Shift+Z).

   This will put back the removed header or footer and all the information it contained. As with the Undo command, if you've restored other changes since you removed the header or footer, you'll have to use the Redo command multiple times.

To edit a header or footer:

1. Choose Document > Add Headers and Footers.

2. Click the Header or Footer tab in the dialog box. The options are the same in either tab.

3. Change any of the settings. To remove custom text, select it and click the Remove button (**Figure 5.33**).

✔ Tip

■ Once you save a PDF file, any headers and footers you have created become just text within the PDF file, like any other text. Among other things, this means that you can no longer edit the headers and footers in the Add Headers & Footers dialog box.

ADDING HEADERS AND FOOTERS

Working with Watermarks and Backgrounds

You can have Acrobat add a graphic to the background or foreground of the pages in your document. This graphic can be a note, a company logo, or anything else you'd like. Acrobat calls this graphic a background if it is placed behind the contents of your pages; the graphic is a watermark if it is placed on top of your pages' contents. The source of this graphic is a page taken from another PDF file.

To add a watermark or background:

1. Choose Document > Add Watermark & Background.

   This opens the Add Watermark & Background dialog box (**Figure 5.34**).

2. In the Type area, choose whether to add a background or a watermark by clicking the appropriate radio button in the Type section.

   Also click the check boxes to display your watermark or background on screen, when printing, or both.

3. Click the Choose button to find the graphic for your watermark or background.

4. In the Open dialog box, navigate to the image you want and click Open.

   The image appears in the preview pane on the right of the Add Watermark & Background dialog box.

5. Choose the pages on which you want the watermark or background displayed.

6. Select the vertical and horizontal alignment, rotation, and opacity of the image.

7. Preview your document in the preview pane (**Figure 5.35**). When you're happy with the effect, click OK.

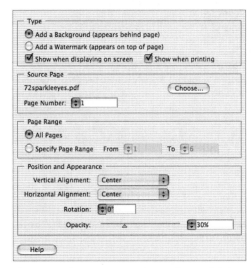

Figure 5.34 The Add Watermark & Background dialog box lets you add and position background graphics on your pages.

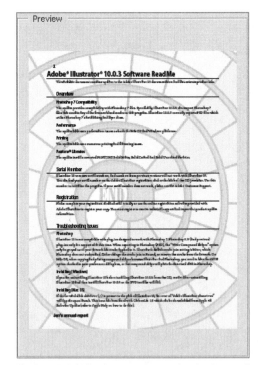

Figure 5.35 Admire the new watermark or background in the preview pane.

✔ Tips

- The vertical and horizontal alignment let you position the background image. If you want it centered, choose Center for both vertical and horizontal alignments.

- If you have trouble seeing the text through the image, lower the opacity setting.

- Although you can apply a background to all pages or a specific page range, it's sometimes most effective to use the background for just the front page.

- To remove a watermark or background you've just added, choose Edit > Undo Add Background or Undo Add Watermark (Ctrl+Z/Command+Z). Use the Redo command (Edit > Add Background or Add Watermark or Ctrl+Shift+Z/Command+Shift+Z) to restore a watermark or background you've just removed.

- Once you save the PDF file, the watermark or background becomes just another set of graphic objects within the PDF file. You can no longer edit, remove, or otherwise manipulate it as a watermark or background.

WORKING WITH WATERMARKS/BACKGROUNDS

Saving PDF Files in Other Formats

With Acrobat 6.0 Standard, reusing the contents of your PDFs in other programs is easy. You can save a PDF in any of these common formats:

- **PDF** (*.PDF) can be read by everyone with Adobe Reader or Acrobat 6.0 Standard or Professional.

- **Encapsulated PostScript** is best if you plan to use the document as an illustration in a page-layout program.

- **HTML** is best if you plan to put your document on the Web.

- **JPEG, JPEG 2000, PNG,** and **TIFF** are all graphics formats that convert each page of the PDF to a separate bitmapped image file. You lose the ability to edit text. These formats are useful for exchanging higher quality graphics and photographs.

- **PostScript** files preserve all structuring information and other parameters encoded by Distiller. PostScript files are often used by programmers who may want to add pieces of special-purpose PostScript to modify the way the document prints.

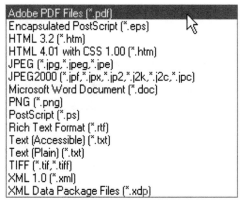

Figure 5.36 From the pop-up menu, choose the format in which you want to save the file.

◆ **Rich Text Format** and **Microsoft Word Document** both allow you to reuse the document's text in a word processor.

◆ **Plain Text** and **Accessible Text** both convert a document to text only, with no formatting. It's useful for reflowing text into another layout or text application. For example, you can take text from an older PDF document and reflow it into a QuarkXPress, InDesign, or PageMaker document.

◆ **XML** and **XML Data Package Files** are used for high-end forms and document management systems, for example, when exchanging data among publishing work-flows.

To save a PDF in another format:

1. Choose Save As from the File menu (Shift+Ctrl+S/Shift+Command+S).

2. In the Save As dialog box, choose the desired format from the pop-up menu (**Figure 5.36**).

3. Click the Settings button to change format-specific parameters for the file (see Acrobat Help for more details).

4. Type a name for the file and choose a location to save it to, then click Save.

   The file is saved in the chosen location with the name you gave it.

SAVING PDF FILES IN OTHER FORMATS

Reducing PDF File Sizes

Sometimes when you're sending files to other users, you need to minimize your file size, making the file as small as possible for transferring. Acrobat can scan through your PDF file, applying a number of strategies to reduce the file's size, while still keeping it readable to a viewer.

To reduce file size:

1. Choose File > Reduce File Size.

This brings up the Reduce File Size dialog box (**Figure 5.37**).

2. From the Compatible With pop-up menu, choose a version of Acrobat you know your recipient can use.

If you aren't sure what version of Acrobat to choose, you should probably go with the oldest.

3. Click OK.

This brings up the Save As dialog box so you can give this reduced file a new name and keep the original intact. You can also choose to replace the original file with the smaller file. In some cases, you can reduce the file size by almost 50 percent this way.

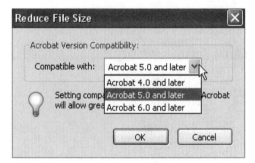

Figure 5.37 Pick the latest version of Acrobat your recipient will be able to open, and click OK.

REDUCING PDF FILE SIZES

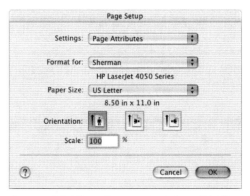

Figure 5.38 Set the options you want, then click OK.

Printing PDFs

Printing a PDF to any printer is fairly straightforward.

To set up printing on a Macintosh:

1. Choose Page Setup from the File menu. This opens the Page Setup dialog box.

2. Choose your printer from the pop-up menu.

3. Choose the Paper size, orientation, and scale (**Figure 5.38**).

4. Click OK to accept your selected options and exit the Page Setup dialog box.

To print on a Macintosh:

1. Choose Print from the File menu to open the Print dialog box.

2. Choose your printer from the pop-up menu.

3. Examine the printing options to see if any of them need adjusting. Most of these are standard settings, but some are unique to Acrobat. You should pay special attention to:

   Print What. Should Acrobat print the document, the document and its comments, or only the contents of form fields? Usually you will want to print the document and its comments.

   Page Scaling. Should Acrobat automatically scale your pages to make sure they fit on the page? Usually, you will select None, which yields the fewest surprises.

   Auto-Rotate and Center. Should Acrobat automatically rotate the pages and center them on the paper for the "best" printing results? Leave this unchecked, as it mostly results in the printed page being different from what you intended.

4. Click the Print button.

PRINTING PDFS

PRINTING PDFs

To set up printing for Windows:

1. Choose Print from the File menu to open the Print dialog box.

2. From the Name pop-up menu, choose the printer that you want to use (**Figure 5.39**).

3. If you want to change any of the printer options, click the Properties button in to display the options for your specific printer (**Figure 5.40**).

4. When you're finished changing the printer options, click OK to return to the Print dialog box.

5. Set the print range, number of copies, and any necessary PostScript options (**Figure 5.41**).

6. Click OK to print the PDF document.

Figure 5.39 Choose your printer from the Name pop-up menu.

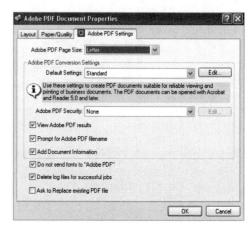

Figure 5.40 Click the Properties button to change printer options.

Figure 5.41 Set the PostScript options you want, then click OK.

STRUCTURING PDF DOCUMENTS

6

PDF documents are ready to go immediately after you create them, but you can do all sorts of things to make the files even more readable and easier to use. Adobe Acrobat provides several options for customizing PDF documents.

This chapter covers some of the changes you can make in PDF files at the page level. When you've finished working with Acrobat, remember to save your documents so that anyone reading them will see the changes you've made.

Getting Information About Your Document

You can find out many things about a PDF document. Choosing Document Properties from the File menu gives you a variety of options (**Figure 6.1**). The main source of information is the document summary. You can also get information on—and change (only in Acrobat Pro or Standard, not Reader)—several other options:

◆ **Advanced** shows the Base URL for relative Web links in your PDF document (**Figure 6.2**). When you specify a base URL, managing the links in the document is easier. You can also find out here whether trapping has been used in the document, which is helpful to any prepress person printing the document. Search Index gives the name of any auto-index that belongs with the document, and adds the index to the existing list of indexes used in a search. Finally, you can see the binding edge and language options specified.

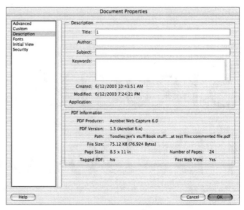

Figure 6.1 Open the Document Properties window to view and change information about a PDF file.

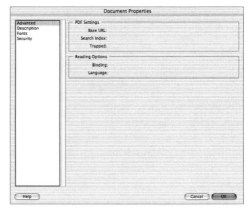

Figure 6.2 The Advanced panel of the Document Properties window is most useful for publishing your PDFs online or in print.

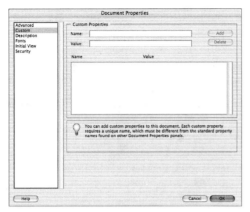

Figure 6.3 The Custom panel of the Document Properties window lets you make a document uniquely yours.

◆ **Custom** lets advanced users add their own properties to the document. This is for the use of custom-written software (**Figure 6.3**).

◆ **Description** contains basic information about the document—author, title, subject, and so on—and uneditable information such as the application that created the document, its creation and modification dates, and the file size.

◆ **Fonts** (Ctrl+Alt+F/Command+Option+F) lists the fonts used in the document.

◆ **Initial View** lets you choose how a PDF document will be displayed when it is opened. You can change how much of the Acrobat interface is visible and the magnification at which it is viewed. See more about these options on the following page.

◆ **Security** displays the permissions for various areas of the document. For more on Security options see Appendix B.

GETTING INFORMATION ABOUT YOUR DOCUMENT

Changing Open Options

By default, both Acrobat 6 and Adobe Reader open PDF files to the first page and at the Fit in Window magnification level. At times, however, you want a document to open to a different page or at a different magnification level. Setting these properties in Document Properties affects only the current document; the same properties can also be set among the Acrobat preferences, in which case they apply to all documents (unless overridden by the document).

To change the way a file opens:

1. Choose File > Document Properties > Initial View.

   The Initial View pane of Document Properties appears (**Figure 6.4**).

2. Make your changes.

   You can specify which page the document will open to and what interface elements will be visible.

3. Click OK.

4. Save the document by choosing File > Save (Ctrl+S/Command+S).

   The next time someone opens the document in Acrobat or Reader, it will look the way you specified.

✔ Tip

■ To set a new magnification level, type a specific value in the Magnification text field or make a selection from the pull-down menu (click the triangle next to the field).

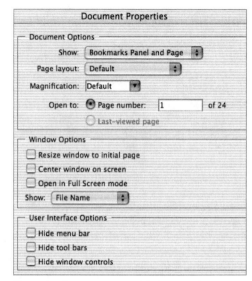

Figure 6.4 The Document Initial View pane lets you choose how your documents open.

Document options for Initial View

In the Initial View pane of Document Properties, you can change settings not only for your pages, but the window it opens in and the entire user interface. These controls allow you to display or hide most parts of the user interface (the toolbars, the menu bar, etc.). But you can't rearrange controls or pick and choose particular toolbar buttons. Here are a few examples:

◆ The Document Options' **Show** pull-down menu provides a choice of showing the Document pane only, the Bookmarks panel and Document pane, or the Pages panel and Document pane.

◆ From the **Show** pull-down menu in the Window Options area, choose what Acrobat will display in the title bar; your choices are the title of the PDF document (as listed in the document summary) or the document's file name.

◆ **Hide window controls** removes the scroll bars and the close and resize boxes from view. You can get these controls back only by unchecking this option, saving the document, and then closing and reopening the document.

CHANGING OPEN OPTIONS

Working with Thumbnails

Thumbnails provide a quick visual method of going to another page. If you are on page 1 and want to get to page 12 quickly, you can just click the thumbnail for page 12. Each thumbnail is a tiny representation of a page. Clicking a thumbnail instantly takes you to that page at the current magnification level.

Thumbnails are not stored in a PDF by default, because they add to the document's file size, but they are generated on the fly when you open the Pages panel. These thumbnails will not be saved when the document is closed, however. If you want to make sure that thumbnails are always present in the document, you can embed them.

To view and use thumbnails:

1. Choose View > Navigation Tabs > Pages (**Figure 6.5**).

   The Pages panel on the left side of the document opens and, after a short delay, displays little pictures of the pages in the vicinity of the current page (**Figure 6.6**).

2. Click the thumbnail for the page you want.

   You move to that page instantly. Acrobat discards the previous thumbnails and generates new ones.

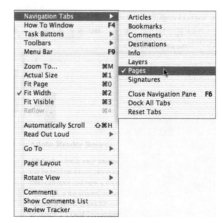

Figure 6.5 Choose View > Navigation Tabs > Pages to display the Pages pane.

Figure 6.6 The Pages pane is displayed on the left side of the application.

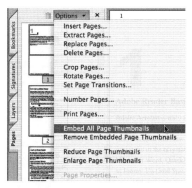

Figure 6.7 Choose Embed All Page Thumbnails from the Pages pane Options pop-up menu.

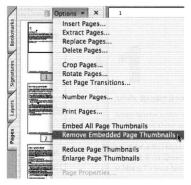

Figure 6.8 To delete thumbnails, choose Remove Embedded Page Thumbnails from the Pages pane Options pop-up menu.

Figure 6.9 This dialog box asks for confirmation before deleting thumbnails.

To embed thumbnails in a document:

1. Choose View > Navigation Tabs > Pages, and click the Pages tab along the left edge of the document.

2. Choose Embed All Page Thumbnails from the Pages pane pop-up menu (**Figure 6.7**).

   Acrobat creates thumbnails for every page in the document and stores them permanently within the PDF. Now thumbnails will be displayed immediately when you move to a different part of the document, rather than after a delay.

To delete thumbnails:

1. Choose Remove Embedded Page Thumbnails from the Pages pane pop-up menu (**Figure 6.8**).

   A dialog box appears, asking whether you're sure that you want to remove the thumbnails.

2. Click OK (**Figure 6.9**).

✔ Tip

- After you edit a PDF document with embedded page thumbnails, you must remove them and then embed a fresh set, so they reflect the changes you made in the document.

WORKING WITH THUMBNAILS

Changing Page Order and Numbers

Shuffling pages around within a PDF document is as simple as dragging and dropping, thanks to the magical goodness of thumbnails.

To reorder pages within a PDF:

1. With the document open and page thumbnails showing, click to select the thumbnail of the page or pages you want to reorder (**Figure 6.10**).

2. Drag to the point where you want to move the page.

   A blue bar marks the spot (**Figure 6.11**).

3. Release the mouse button to drop the pages in their new location.

   The pages are renumbered to accommodate the move (**Figure 6.12**).

✔ Tips

■ Hold down Ctrl+Alt/Command+Option while dragging to move a copy of the selected pages to the new location, while the original pages remain in place.

■ You may select and move a group of nonconsecutive pages, but they will be consecutive after you drop the pages in their new location.

Figure 6.10 Select the thumbnails of the pages you'd like to move.

Figure 6.11 A blue bar marks the destination for your pages.

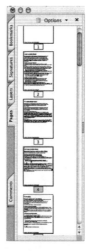

Figure 6.12 The moved pages are now in their new location.

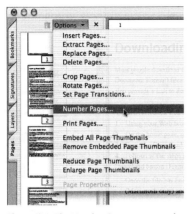

Figure 6.13 The Number Pages command is in the Pages pane Options pop-up menu.

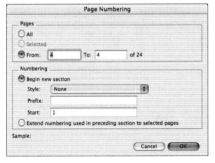

Figure 6.14 The Page Numbering dialog box offers many choices for custom numbering schemes.

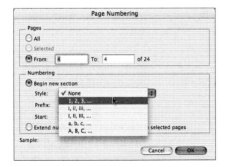

Figure 6.15 Choose a numbering style.

By default, Acrobat numbers document pages consecutively, starting from 1, using Arabic numerals. Occasionally, you may want to impose a custom page-numbering scheme on a document. You may want to number front-matter pages with Roman numerals, for example, or number the pages within each chapter separately.

To renumber pages:

1. Choose Number Pages from the Pages panel Options menu (**Figure 6.13**).

   The Page Numbering dialog box opens (**Figure 6.14**).

2. Choose which pages you want to renumber: All, Selected, or a range of pages.

3. If you want to continue the same numbering that was used in the preceding section, click the Extend Numbering Used radio button.

   or

   If you want to use a new sequence of numbers in these pages, click Begin new section; then choose a numbering style from the pop-up menu (**Figure 6.15**), a prefix for the page numbers (if desired), and a number to start the sequence.

✔ Tips

- If you prefer to see the default numbering system in Pages panel and status bar rather than your custom numbering system, uncheck Use Logical Page Numbers in the Page Display area of the Preferences dialog box (Ctrl+K/Command+K).

- These page numbers will appear in the Window Controls at the bottom of the document window, not as numbers on the document's pages.

CHANGING PAGE ORDER AND NUMBERS

Inserting and Replacing PDF Pages

Often, you want to move pages from one document to another or combine multiple PDFs into a single document. Acrobat provides two ways to accomplish these tasks. One method involves menu commands; the other requires you simply to drag page thumbnails around.

To insert one PDF document into another:

1. While you have a document open, choose Document > Pages > Insert Pages (Ctrl+Shift+I/Command+Shift+I), or choose Insert Pages from the Pages palette Options menu (**Figure 6.16**). The Select File to Insert dialog box appears (**Figure 6.17**).

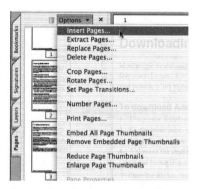

Figure 6.16 To insert pages into a file, choose Insert Pages from the Pages pane Options menu.

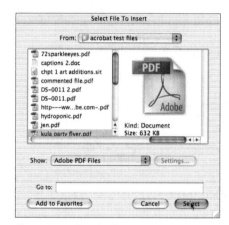

Figure 6.17 Select the file you want to insert.

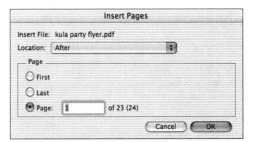

Figure 6.18 Specify where you want to insert the file.

2. Navigate to the file you'd like to insert into the current document, then click Select.

   The Insert Pages dialog box appears (**Figure 6.18**).

3. In the Page portion of the dialog box, specify where you want the pages to be inserted.

   Click the First or Last radio button, or type a number in the Page text field.

4. From the Location menu, choose whether the document will be inserted before or after the page you chose.

5. Click OK.

   The pages will be inserted at the document location you selected.

✔ Tip

■ If you don't want to insert the entire contents of a file, you'll have to open that file and extract the pages you want to insert in a new file. (Extracting pages is explained later in this chapter.) Be sure to use a distinctive name for the file that contains the extracted pages, so you don't confuse it with the whole document.

To replace one PDF page with another:

1. Start with a document in which you want to place new pages.

2. Choose Document > Pages > Replace Pages, or choose Replace Pages from the Pages palette Options menu (**Figure 6.19**).

   The Select File with New Pages dialog box appears.

3. Select the file that contains the replacement pages; then click Select (**Figure 6.20**).

   The Replace Pages dialog box appears.

4. In the text fields in the Original section (**Figure 6.21**), type the page numbers of the range of pages you want to replace in the open document.

   This range determines the number of pages that will be taken from the replacement document. You can replace only the same number of pages.

5. In the Replacement text field, type the number of the first replacement page.

   Acrobat automatically calculates the range of pages needed to replace the pages you have chosen in the original file. Click OK.

6. A warning will appear asking if you really want to replace those pages. Click Yes.

   The specified pages of the open document are replaced.

✔ Tip

■ You'll have to replace noncontiguous pages separately. To insert pages 1 and 5 from a replacement document, for example, you'll need to perform the Replace Pages process twice.

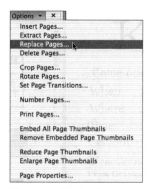

Figure 6.19 The Replace Pages command is in the Options menu.

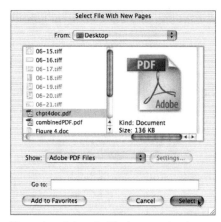

Figure 6.20 Select the file that contains the replacement pages.

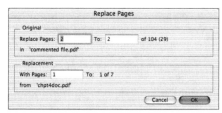

Figure 6.21 Indicate which pages you want replaced, as well as the pages that will replace them.

INSERTING AND REPLACING PDF PAGES

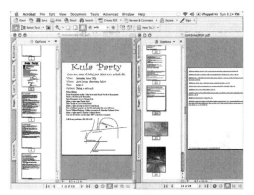

Figure 6.22 Line up the two documents side by side with their Navigation panes open.

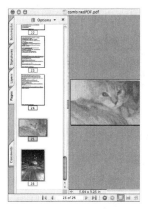

Figure 6.23 Select pages to copy to the other document.

Figure 6.24 Drag pages from the source document's Navigation pane to the original's.

Moving pages as thumbnails

You'll usually find that page thumbnails provide an easier way to move individual pages between PDFs.

To copy pages from one document to another:

1. Open both the document into which you want to copy pages (the original document) and the document from which you want to copy pages (the source document).

2. Open the Navigation panel of each window and arrange them so that both documents are visible, with the source document on top (**Figure 6.22**).

3. In the source document, select the thumbnails of the pages you want to copy. (Shift-click to select consecutive pages; Ctrl-click/Command-click to select nonconsecutive pages.)

   A faint blue outline appears around the selected pages (**Figure 6.23**).

4. Drag the selected page thumbnails into the Pages palette of the original document.

   The mouse pointer changes to an arrow (**Figure 6.24**).

(continues on next page)

INSERTING AND REPLACING PDF PAGES

5. Release the mouse button over the spot where you want to insert the pages.

As the mouse moves over a spot between pages, a blue bar appears. The pages are copied from the source document to the original document, and the pages in the original document are renumbered (**Figure 6.25**).

✔ Tips

■ To move pages from one document to another, follow the same procedure, but hold down Ctrl+Alt/Command+Option while dragging. This method inserts the page into the original document and removes it from the source document. Afterward, pages in both documents are renumbered.

■ This method works only when the Pages pane is docked, not floating. For more information on docked and floating panes, see Chapter 1.

To replace one PDF page with another:

1. Display the Pages panels of both the source and original documents.

2. In the source document, select the thumbnails of the replacement pages.

3. Drag the selected thumbnails into the Pages pane of the original document, positioning the mouse pointer over the page number of the first page you want to replace.

The pages that will be replaced turn black (**Figure 6.26**).

4. Release the mouse button.

The pages from the source document replace an equal number of pages in the original document (**Figure 6.27**).

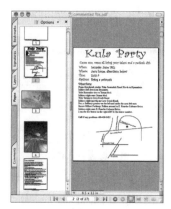

Figure 6.25 The pages are copied, and page numbers are recalculated.

Figure 6.26 Drag the replacement pages' thumbnails into the Pages palette of the original document.

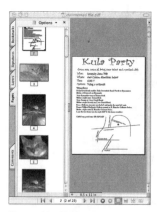

Figure 6.27 The pages are replaced.

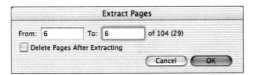

Figure 6.28 Enter the pages to remove in the Extract Pages dialog box.

Removing PDF Pages

You can export selected pages from a PDF document to a new document. You can also use this process—called "extracting" in Acrobat—to remove pages as you export them. In effect, extracting breaks a PDF document into smaller documents.

To extract pages from a PDF document:

1. Choose Document > Pages > Extract Pages, or choose Extract Pages from the Pages palette Options menu.

    The Extract Pages dialog box appears (**Figure 6.28**).

2. In the text fields, type the page numbers of the page or range of pages you want to extract from the active document.

    Alternatively, select the thumbnails of the pages you want to extract before using the command. The range you selected will be displayed in the dialog box.

3. If you want Acrobat to delete the extracted pages from the document, make sure that the Delete Pages After Extracting check box is checked.

4. Click OK.

    A new document containing the extracted pages opens. This new document is automatically named "Pages from [original document name]." The document has not been saved at this point, so be sure to rename and save it before closing the file or exiting Acrobat.

Although you can use extracting to remove pages from a PDF document, the process also creates a new document that you may not need. Sometimes, you just want to get rid of pages. Acrobat lets you do so with the Delete Pages command.

To delete pages from a PDF document:

1. Choose Document > Pages > Delete Pages (Ctrl+Shift+D/Command+Shift+D), or choose Delete Pages from the Pages pane Options pop-up menu.

   The Delete Pages dialog box appears (**Figure 6.29**).

2. In the text fields, type the page numbers of the page or range of pages you want to delete.

3. Click OK.

   A dialog box appears, asking whether you're sure that you want to delete the specified pages (**Figure 6.30**).

4. If you are sure, click Yes.

   The pages will be deleted.

✔ Tip

- You can delete pages from a PDF document using the page thumbnails. Select the thumbnails of the pages you want to delete and then press Backspace or Delete. When the confirmation dialog box appears, click Yes to delete the pages.

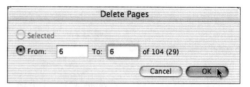

Figure 6.29 Specify which pages you want to delete.

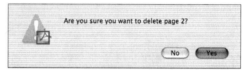

Figure 6.30 Click Yes if you're sure you want to delete the pages.

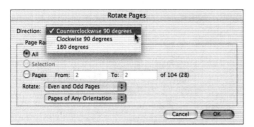

Figure 6.31 In the Rotate Pages dialog box, specify the pages to be rotated and the direction of the rotation.

Rotating and Cropping Pages

Occasionally, a PDF page will be rotated the wrong way when it opens in Acrobat. You can fix that in the Rotate Pages dialog box.

To rotate a PDF page:

1. Choose Document > Pages > Rotate (Ctrl+Shift+R/Command+Shift+R), or choose Rotate from the Pages palette Options pop-up menu.

The Rotate Pages dialog box appears.

2. Specify the direction and amount you want to rotate the pages (**Figure 6.31**).

3. Specify the page or range of pages to be rotated.

You can use the pop-up menus at the bottom of the dialog box to narrow your choice of pages, for example, rotating only even pages or only pages currently in landscape orientation.

4. Click OK.

The pages are rotated.

✔ Tip

■ To rotate several sets of noncontiguous pages, you'll have to handle each contiguous set separately.

ROTATING AND CROPPING PAGES

105

PDF pages created in a different application (such as Microsoft Word, Adobe Illustrator, or Adobe Photoshop) may contain areas that you don't need. Acrobat provides a convenient way to crop out these areas.

To crop a PDF page:

1. Choose Document > Pages > Crop (Ctrl+Shift+T/Command+Shift+T), or choose Crop from the Pages panel Options pop-up menu (**Figure 6.32**).

   or

   Click the Crop tool in the Advanced Editing toolbar, drag across the page to define the boundaries of the crop, and press Enter or Return. If the Crop tool is not visible, choose View > Toolbars > Advanced Editing and the Advanced Editing toolbar with the Crop tool will appear as a floating palette (**Figure 6.33**).

   Whichever method you use, the Crop Pages dialog box appears (**Figure 6.34**).

Figure 6.32 To crop pages you can use the command in the Pages palette's Options menu...

Figure 6.33 ...or the Crop tool in the Advanced Editing toolbar.

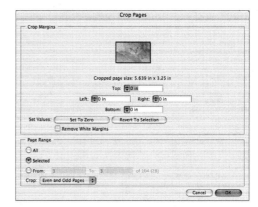

Figure 6.34 In the Crop Pages dialog box, enter numbers for the new margins and specify which pages will be cropped.

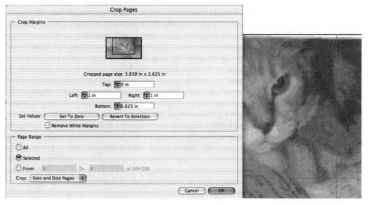

Figure 6.35 Dotted lines in the Document pane show where your cropping will occur.

ROTATING AND CROPPING PAGES

2. In the Crop Margins text fields, type the amount you want to crop from each page edge (or select the distances by clicking the up and down arrows by each box).

   As you change these numbers, a black line appears on the document thumbnail at the center of the dialog box, giving you a preview of the new margins. At the same time, a dotted line appears on the document at each of the margins being cropped (**Figure 6.35**).

3. If you don't like what you've chosen and want to start over, click the Set to Zero button to remove all changes.

   If you previously defined a cropping area with the Crop tool and then changed it in the dialog box, you can return to the original selection by clicking the Revert to Selection button.

4. In the Page Range section, select the pages to be cropped.

   In addition to cropping every page or only selected pages, you can crop only even or odd pages by selecting that from the Crop pop-up menu.

5. Click OK.

   A dialog box appears, asking whether you really want to crop the selected pages.

6. Click Yes to crop the pages as you've indicated, or click No to leave the document untouched.

✔ Tip

■ You cannot undo a cropping action, but if you choose Revert from the File menu, Acrobat will revert to the last saved version of the PDF document. Keep in mind that if you save and reopen the document later, you have no way to retrieve the areas that you've cropped, even if you use the Revert command.

ROTATING AND CROPPING PAGES

Creating and Viewing Bookmarks

Most authors of multiple-page PDFs add bookmarks to their documents to provide the reader quick access to specific passages. But you can set up bookmarks to do more than just take the reader to a specific page in a document. You can also customize a bookmark to display a page at a certain magnification or direct the reader's attention to a specific part of the page.

The most helpful kind of bookmark reflects the structure of the document. Because it's possible to arrange bookmarks in hierarchies, you could construct a detailed table of contents out of bookmarks (see the bookmarks in the Acrobat Help file for an outstanding example).

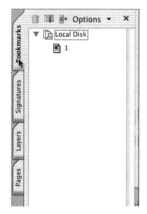

Figure 6.36 Click the tab on the left side of the window to open the Bookmarks pane.

To display the Bookmarks pane:

◆ Choose View > Navigation tabs > Bookmarks.

 or

 Click the Bookmarks tab on the left side of the Navigation pane (**Figure 6.36**).

To use a bookmark:

1. Open the Bookmarks pane to display all the bookmarks available for the active document.

2. Click the bookmark you want to go to. The Document pane changes to show the bookmarked page.

Figure 6.37 Select the bookmark after which you'd like to add the new bookmark.

Figure 6.38 Click the Create New Bookmark icon at the top of the Bookmarks pane.

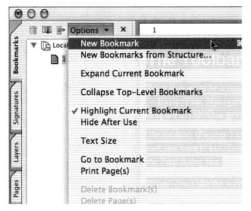

Figure 6.39 Choose New Bookmark from the Bookmarks pane's Options menu.

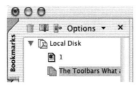

Figure 6.40 The new Bookmark will appear right where you designated it should be.

To create a bookmark:

1. In your current document, display the Bookmarks pane.

2. If your document already contains bookmarks, click to select the bookmark after which you want to add the new one (**Figure 6.37**).

3. Navigate to the spot in your document that you want to bookmark.

4. Zoom into the desired magnification at the spot on the page where you want to direct the reader's attention.

5. Use the Text Select tool to select the text that will be the bookmark.

6. Click the Create New Bookmark icon (**Figure 6.38**) at the top of the Bookmarks pane (it looks like a book with a red bookmark in the center).

   or

   Choose New Bookmark (Ctrl+B/ Command+B) from the Bookmarks pane Options pop-up menu (**Figure 6.39**).

   A new bookmark appears in the Bookmarks pane (**Figure 6.40**).

Moving Bookmarks

Suppose that you mistakenly created a bookmark that took the reader to the middle of a page instead of to the top. Rather than delete it and start over, you can simply change its destination.

By default, bookmarks appear in the palette in the order in which you create them. If you like, you can change that order or reorganize a long list of bookmarks into a more useful hierarchical list. For example, you may want to define one page as a main heading, or *parent* bookmark, and another as a subheading, or *child* bookmark.

To change the destination of a bookmark:

1. Open a PDF document and display the Bookmarks pane.

2. Click to select the bookmark whose destination you want to change.

3. Move to the new target location in the document.

4. Choose Set Bookmark Destination from the Bookmarks pane's Options pop-up menu (**Figure 6.41**).

   A warning dialog box appears, asking if you're sure you want to change the bookmark's destination.

5. Click Yes to reset the bookmark (**Figure 6.42**).

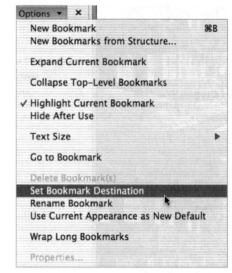

Figure 6.41 Choose Set Bookmark Destination from the Bookmarks palette's Options menu.

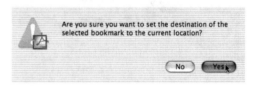

Figure 6.42 Click Yes to reset the bookmark's destination.

MOVING BOOKMARKS

Figure 6.43 Move a bookmark by dragging it up or down in the list.

Figure 6.44 Make a child bookmark by dragging it up or down in the list. A line shows where the bookmark will land.

Figure 6.45 When the child bookmark is in place, it appears below the parent bookmark and indented.

To move a bookmark within the list:

1. Click to select the bookmark you want to move.

2. Drag the bookmark up or down in the list.

   As the mouse pointer passes over a space between two bookmarks, a red line appears in the space, showing you where the dragged bookmark will be placed if you release the mouse button (**Figure 6.43**).

3. Release the mouse button when you reach the desired location of the bookmark.

   The bookmark appears in its new location.

To place a bookmark within another bookmark:

1. Click to select the bookmark you intend to define as a child.

2. Drag the bookmark until the mouse pointer is over the *name* of the bookmark (not the bookmark itself) that you want to define as the parent bookmark.

   A red line appears, showing where the dragged bookmark will be moved (**Figure 6.44**).

3. Release the mouse button.

   The dragged bookmark is now hierarchically below the bookmark to which it was dragged, and that bookmark is now its parent (**Figure 6.45**). The parent bookmark is identified by a plus sign (Windows) or triangle (Mac OS) to its left. Clicking this symbol reveals the child bookmarks below the parent in the hierarchy.

MOVING BOOKMARKS

Changing Bookmark Properties

Reading through a long list of bookmarks can be a bit mind-numbing. You can alter the appearance of bookmarks to make the hierarchy more visible and easier to navigate. For example, make all chapter headings bold and italic, and make all figure references red text.

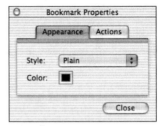

Figure 6.46 Set bookmark properties in the Bookmark Properties dialog box.

To change a bookmark's properties:

1. Open the Bookmarks pane for the current document.

2. Click to select a bookmark.

3. Choose Properties from the Bookmarks pane's Options pop-up menu.

   The Bookmark Properties dialog box appears (**Figure 6.46**). Choose the Appearance tab.

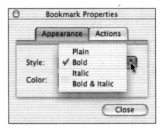

Figure 6.47 Choose a new color and style for the bookmark's name.

4. To change the color or text style of the bookmark's name, click the color box or choose a style from the pop-up menu (**Figure 6.47**) in the Appearance section of the dialog box.

5. Click Close.

CHANGING BOOKMARK PROPERTIES

Figure 6.48 Choose the Article tool in the toolbar.

Figure 6.49 The article is indicated by a box topped by a number.

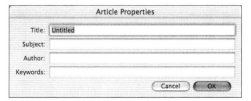

Figure 6.50 After you create an article, you can use the Article Properties dialog box to add information about the article.

Creating Articles

If your document contains stories that appear on different parts of a page or several pages, as often happens in newspapers and magazines, you can define articles within the document, to guide the reader through the story from beginning to end. Use the Article tool to link the various parts of the text so that the reader will be able to follow the flow of the story.

To create an article:

1. Open the document in which you want to create the article.

2. Click the Article tool in the Advanced Editing toolbar (**Figure 6.48**).

   If the toolbar isn't visible, choose View > Toolbars > Advanced Editing.

3. Drag the Article tool across the section of text you want to define as the first part of the article.

   When you release the mouse button, the text is numbered and surrounded by a box (**Figure 6.49**). The article numbers show you this article's sequence in the document and this section's sequence in the article.

4. Drag the Article tool to select the next section of text that you want to link to the first one.

   This section of the article will be labeled 1-2; subsequent sections will be labeled 1-3, 1-4, and so on.

5. Choose View > Navigation tabs > Articles to see the Articles pane and the list of articles.

6. Double-click an article in the pane to give it a title, subject, author, and keywords in the Article Properties dialog box (**Figure 6.50**).

To extend an article:

1. Click the Article tool.

   All articles in the document are displayed.

2. Click the section of the article to which you want to add material.

3. Click the bottom-right corner and drag it out to include more text (**Figure 6.51**).

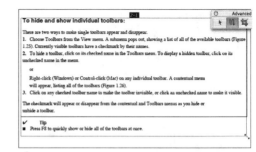

Figure 6.51 Drag out the corner box of an article to extend the article.

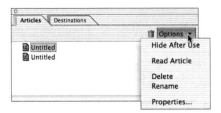

Figure 6.52 Choose Rename from the pane menu to change an article's name.

Editing Articles

After you create articles in a PDF document, you can rename them, add or remove sections of text, combine articles into a single article, or delete articles from the document.

To rename an article:

1. Choose View > Navigation tabs > Articles to display the Articles pane.

   All the articles in the document are listed.

2. Click to select an article and choose Rename from the Articles pane's Options pop-up menu (**Figure 6.52**), or double-click the article's name.

3. Type a new name and then press Enter or Return.

To combine articles:

1. Click the Article tool.

2. Click the first article to be combined (**Figure 6.53**).

3. Click the plus sign in the bottom-right corner of the article box (**Figure 6.54**). You must be sure to click exactly once on the little plus sign. It's a little disconcerting, because Acrobat gives you no indication that anything special has happened when you click on the plus sign.

4. Press Ctrl (Windows) or Option (Macintosh), and click the box you want to combine with the first article (**Figure 6.55**).

   The two articles are now attached and can be read one after the other. Any other articles are renumbered.

Figure 6.53 To combine articles, first click the initial portion...

Figure 6.54 ...then click the plus sign in the bottom-right corner.

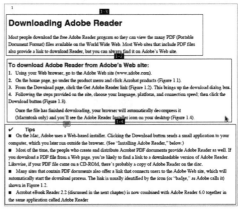

Figure 6.55 Ctrl-click or Option-click the second article to join it to the first one.

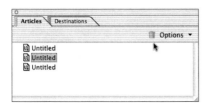

Figure 6.56 Click the Trash icon to delete the selected articles.

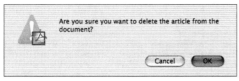

Figure 6.57 Acrobat asks if you really want to delete the articles.

To remove an article:

1. In the Articles panel, click the article that you want to remove.

2. Click the Trash icon in the Articles panel (**Figure 6.56**).

or

Press Backspace or Delete.

A dialog box appears, asking whether you're sure that you want to delete the article (**Figure 6.57**).

3. Click OK to remove the article.

EDITING ARTICLES

Reading Articles

To read all the parts of an article through to the end, just follow the pointer.

To read an article:

1. Open the Articles palette. The Articles palette isn't visible by default; you need to select it from View > Navigation Panels > Articles.

2. Double-click the article that you want to read. The cursor automatically becomes the Follow Article cursor when you double-click the article (**Figure 6.58**).

   You are taken to the start of the article.

3. Click or press Enter or Return repeatedly to advance through the article; Shift-click or press Shift+Enter or Shift+Return to go backward.

   When you reach the end of the article, the mouse pointer changes to the End Article pointer. Click to go back to the view you had of the document before you started to read the article.

✔ Tips

■ While you're reading an article, Ctrl-click or Option-click at any time to return to the start of the article.

■ The hand cursor will *always* turn into the Follow Article cursor when it passes over an article on the page, whether or not you have the Articles palette visible.

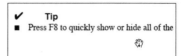

> ✔ **Tip**
> ■ Press F8 to quickly show or hide all of the

Figure 6.58 The Follow Article pointer is displayed while you're reading the article.

READING ARTICLES

Figure 6.59 Choose Create PDF from Multiple Files to begin creating a slide show.

Figure 6.60 Choose a file you want to add and click the Add button.

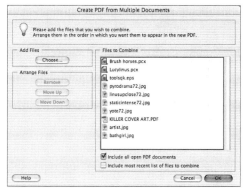

Figure 6.61 Make sure all of the files you want are in the Files to Combine area, and in the correct order.

Creating a Slide Show

One of the less-known features of Acrobat is its capacity to create a slide show. You can create an art gallery, a photo exhibit, or a business presentation with charts, graphs, and other fancy features. I like to create slideshows of my artwork so that I have a reference gallery. One really fantastic thing about using Acrobat to create a presentation is that you can then send it to anyone over the Internet and it's virtually guaranteed that they'll be able to open and view it.

To create a slide show:

1. Choose the documents you want to display in the slide show, and convert them to PDF documents (if necessary) or to any of the graphic-file formats that Acrobat can import. You can convert HTML Text, and numerous graphics format files into PDF files with Acrobat.

2. Choose File > Create PDF > From Multiple Files (**Figure 6.59**). See Chapter 4 if you need a refresher on preparing your files for becoming PDFs.

   The Create PDF from Multiple Documents dialog box appears.

3. In the Add Files area, click the Choose button to select a file for the slide show. The Open dialog box appears.

4. Choose the file you want to convert to a PDF and click the Add button (**Figure 6.60**).

   The file is now listed in the Files to Combine area of the Create PDF from Multiple Documents dialog box.

5. Repeat steps 3 and 4 until all the files you want in the slide show appear in the Files to Combine area (**Figure 6.61**).

(continues on next page)

6. Click OK to combine all of the files into one PDF document.

The progress window appears, showing you Acrobat's progress in combining the files (**Figure 6.62**).

7. Save the combined file.

8. Open the Preferences dialog box by choosing File > Preferences (on a Mac, Acrobat > Preferences), or by pressing Ctrl+K/Command+K.

9. Click the Full Screen preferences (**Figure 6.63**) to begin making your PDF into a slide show.

10. Set the Full Screen Navigation options to determine whether your slides advance automatically or when you click, whether it goes back to the beginning when finished, and how to exit the slide show.

11. Under the Full Screen Appearance area, click the Ignore all transitions check box, or choose from a variety of transitions to go from one slide to the next (**Figure 6.64**).

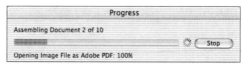

Figure 6.62 The Progress bar displays how far along the combining of files is.

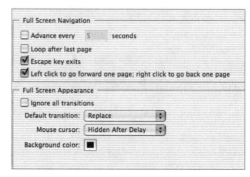

Figure 6.63 Choose Full Screen in the Preferences dialog box to set the slide show preferences.

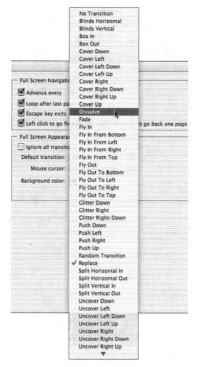

Figure 6.64 Set the transitions for the whole slide show.

CREATING A SLIDE SHOW

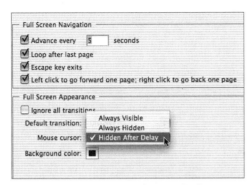

Figure 6.65 Set the mouse preferences for the slide show.

Figure 6.66 Press Ctrl+L or Command+L to activate the slide show. Press the same again to stop the slide show.

12. Choose the mouse cursor visibility from the pop-up menu (**Figure 6.65**).

13. Set the Background color.

14. Click OK to accept these preferences for your slide show.

15. To activate the slide show, press Ctrl+L/Command+L), or choose Window > Full Screen (**Figure 6.66**).

16. To stop the slide show, exit full-screen mode (press the Esc key or Ctrl+L/ Command+L).

If you select "Open in Full Screen mode" in the Initial View properties, the next time you open the file, it will go to full-screen slide-show mode automatically. Exit full-screen mode to return to the Acrobat window.

✔ Tips

- You can add slides to your presentation using the methods covered in "Inserting and Replacing PDF Pages," earlier in this chapter.

- You can use any of the many kinds of files Acrobat can read when creating your slide show. Spice up your presentation with art files, images, charts, and graphs.

CREATING A SLIDE SHOW

Working with Links

Acrobat lets users go instantly from a particular spot in a document to nearly any other location, whether that location is on the same page, in the same document, in a different document, or even on the World Wide Web. Acrobat provides the tools to create links that give users one-click access to other locations.

Links can lead not only to other locations in PDF documents, but also (like bookmarks) to files created by other applications, to forms, JavaScript commands, Web sites, and to multimedia files such as sounds and movies.

Setting Links

Links are great for jumping to other spots in your documents, and they're very easy to create using Acrobat's Link tool. Links can be very obvious or hidden within the document, appearing only when the mouse pointer passes over the link.

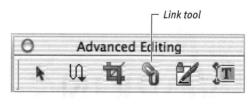

Figure 7.1 Choose the Link tool from the Advanced Editing toolbar.

To link one spot in a PDF document to another:

1. Open the document in which you want to create the link, and go to the page where the link will be.

2. Choose the Link tool from the Advanced Editing toolbar (**Figure 7.1**).

   If the Advanced Editing toolbar is not visible, choose View > Toolbars > Advanced Editing.

Figure 7.2 Drag a marquee around the area that will make up the link.

3. Drag a rectangular marquee around the area you want to define as a link (**Figure 7.2**).

   When you release the mouse button, the Create Link dialog box appears (**Figure 7.3**). You can move this dialog box out of your way (but don't close it) when setting the location of the link.

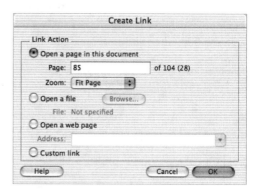

Figure 7.3 Choose a Link Action in the Create Link dialog box, and set other link parameters.

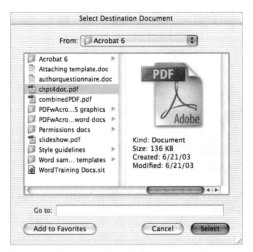

Figure 7.4 Choose another PDF file or even a file in another program.

4. Click the Open a Page in this Document radio button, and enter the number of the page you want to go to.

5. From the Zoom pop-up menu, choose the magnification level at which you want to view the linked page.

6. Click OK to set the link.

The link will work whenever the Hand tool is active. To test the link, navigate back to it and click it with the Hand tool. The linked-to location appears.

✔ Tips

- To link to a page in another PDF document, click the Open a File radio button; this lets you use the Browse button then select a file on your computer.

- To use a link to open a non-Acrobat file or even another application, click the Open a File radio button; then click the Browse button and navigate to the document or application you want the link to open (**Figure 7.4**).

- The Custom Link option lets the user associate a link with an action: execute a JavaScript, submit a form, and so on.

Linking to the Internet

As mentioned earlier in this chapter, links can connect to locations outside Acrobat, as far as the Internet can reach. If the text of your PDF document contains URLs that you would like to act as links to the Internet, you can also convert them to Web links.

To link to a Web site:

1. Open the document in which you want to create the link, and go to the page where the link will be.

2. Choose the Link tool from the Advanced Editing toolbar.

3. Drag a marquee around the area you want to define as a link.

   When you release the mouse button, the Create Link dialog box appears.

4. Click the Open a Web Page radio button in the Create Link dialog box (**Figure 7.5**).

5. In the Address field, type the URL of the Web site to which you want to link (**Figure 7.6**) and click OK.

✔ Tip

- If you want your readers to be able to download the contents of the URL into an Acrobat document, you must give the complete address, including http://.

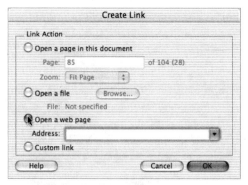

Figure 7.5 Link to the Web by choosing the Web Page radio button in the Create Link dialog box.

Figure 7.6 Enter a URL for the link.

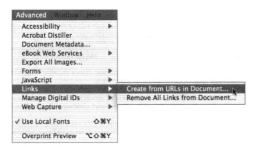

Figure 7.7 Turn all your text URLs into Web links at the same time.

Figure 7.8 Choose whether to convert the entire document or only part of it.

To convert multiple URLs to Web links automatically:

1. Choose Advanced > Links > Create from URLs in Document (**Figure 7.7**).

   The Create Web Links dialog box opens (**Figure 7.8**).

2. Choose whether to generate links on all pages or in a range of pages.

   Acrobat sifts through the pages you specify, searching for URLs, which it converts to Web links. Unfortunately, the process will often miss URLs in the text, so you should go through and make sure all the links were successfully created.

✔ Tips

- The Web links are invisible initially. To find them, choose the Link tool from the Advanced Editing toolbar; then select each Web link to set its properties.

- URLs must be contained within a single line of text for the command to find them. They must also include the protocol prefix (such as http:// or ftp://) to be recognized as URLs.

LINKING TO THE INTERNET

To set the properties of a Web link:

1. Using the Link tool, select a Web link (**Figure 7.9**).

2. Right-click/Control-click to activate the contextual menu.

3. Choose Properties (**Figure 7.10**).
   The Link Properties dialog box appears.

4. To change the appearance of the Web link, click the Appearance tab and select Visible Rectangle from the Link Type, or make any other changes you want.

5. Click the Close button to accept these changes (**Figure 7.11**).

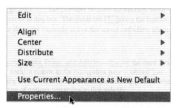

Figure 7.9 To set a link's properties, right-click/Control-click it with the Link tool.

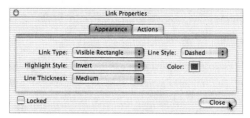

Figure 7.10 Select Properties from the contextual menu.

Figure 7.11 The Link Properties dialog box appears, and you can make all the changes you like.

Figure 7.12 Choose how you'd like to open Web links.

Figure 7.13 A W on the hand pointer means that your Web browser will open the link.

To follow a Web link:

1. Open the document containing the links.

2. Choose the Hand tool from the Basic Tools toolbar.

3. Click the Web link.

   The first time you click any Web link, you'll see the Specify Weblink Behavior dialog box (**Figure 7.12**).

4. Specify whether you want to open Web links in Acrobat or in your Web browser.

   If you choose the In Acrobat radio button, Acrobat attempts to download the Web pages at the URL, convert them to PDF, and append them to the current document. If you choose the In Web Browser radio button, your default browser will open and display the Web page when the link is clicked. So it's safer to choose Web Browser, or you may find yourself adding thousands of pages to your document.

   When the mouse pointer passes over the next link, a tiny symbol appears on the hand image, depending on the Web Capture setting in Acrobat's Preferences (see Chapter 4 for more on this). A *W* signifies that your Web browser will open the link (**Figure 7.13**), and a plus sign means that Acrobat will open the link.

✔ Tip

■ Set Web Capture preferences by choosing Edit (Acrobat in Mac OS X) > Preferences > Web Capture.

Editing Links

After you set a link, you may decide that it should have a different appearance or should perform a different action. And of course, if it's a Web link, it's quite likely (given the fluid nature of the Web) that the site will change or disappear sometime. Fortunately, editing or deleting a link is as easy as setting it up.

To edit an existing link:

1. With the document open to the page that contains the link, choose the Link tool from the Advanced Editing toolbar.

2. Double-click an existing link.

   or

   Right-click/Control-click the link and choose Properties from the contextual menu.

   The outline of the link is displayed along with the Link Properties dialog box (**Figure 7.14**).

3. Change options using the pop-up menus in the Appearance tab or the Actions tab (**Figure 7.15**).

   In Actions tab, click the URL and choose the Edit button. This brings up the Edit URL dialog box (**Figure 7.16**). Enter a new address and click OK, then close the Properties dialog box for the changes to take effect.

   In the Appearance section, choose the appearance you want your link to have, whether a rectangle that stands out from the surrounding text, or no distinguishing features whatsoever.

   In the Actions tab you can select Open a Web link, Go to a Page, Play a Sound, Submit a Form, and other actions.

4. Click OK to set the link changes.

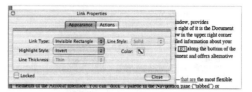

Figure 7.14 The outline of the link appears, along with the Link Properties dialog box.

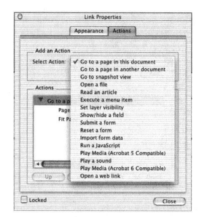

Figure 7.15 A link can perform any of the actions in the Actions tab.

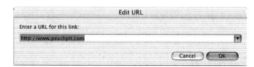

Figure 7.16 Change the URL that your link is tied to.

Figure 7.17 The Appearance properties can make the link can look like a button.

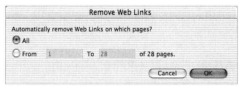

Figure 7.18 Press the Delete/Backspace key to delete the links.

Add a Link for Downloading Acrobat Reader

If you want visitors to your Web site to be able to download Adobe Reader 6 so they can read your PDF documents, you can install a link to Adobe that starts a download of Reader. Follow these steps:

1. In your HTML editor, type this line:

   ```
   <A HREF = "http://www.adobe.com/
   products/acrobat/readstep2.html">
   ```

2. On the next line, type the words that you want to use as the link, such as the following:

   ```
   Click here to download Adobe
   Reader
   ```

3. On the last line, type </A> to tell the browser that it has reached the end of the hyperlinked text.

To set a link's appearance:

1. With the Link tool, right-click/Control-click the link and choose Properties from the contextual menu. This brings up the link's Properties dialog box.

2. Choose Visible Rectangle from the Link Type pop-up menu.

3. Choose Inset from the Highlight Style pop-up menu.

4. Click the Close button to activate these settings.

   Use the Hand tool to see the link, which now looks something like a button (**Figure 7.17**).

To delete a link:

1. Choose the Link tool from the Advanced Editing toolbox.

2. Click the link you want to delete.

   The outline of the link is displayed.

3. Press the Backspace or Delete key.

   or

   Choose Edit > Delete.

   The link is removed.

To delete all Web links:

1. Choose Advanced > Links > Remove All Web Links from Document.

   The Remove Web Links dialog box appears (**Figure 7.18**).

2. Specify whether to delete Web links from all pages or a range of pages.

3. Click OK.

EDITING LINKS

8

Adding Comments

Acrobat 6 ships with a variety of tools that you can use to mark up PDF documents. Using these tools, you can highlight and underline text, include notes, stamps, file attachments, and sound comments, and much more.

You can use comments to request changes in a document, or to call attention to important areas. In addition, you can filter out the comments you don't want to see, so that only the markings relevant to you appear. You can also create a document that summarizes all the comments made in a document.

Understanding the Types of Comments

Some of the Commenting and Advanced Commenting tools are new to Acrobat 6.0. You can access the Commenting and Advanced Commenting toolbars (**Figure 8.1**) from the View > Toolbars submenu. Acrobat offers several types of comments, each designed for a specific type of task:

◆ **Notes** are collapsible text boxes that contain information about a specific area in a document (**Figure 8.2**). Although notes can exist by themselves, most other types of comments, like highlights or cross-outs can be expanded to include notes to further explain the comment

◆ **Text Edits** are comments applied directly to the text of a PDF, including everything from inserting text and notes to highlighting and underlining (**Figure 8.3**). You'll find all the Text Edits in their own pull-down menu in the Commenting toolbar, as well as a command to turn on and off the visibility of Text Edits (**Figure 8.4**).

Figure 8.1 The Commenting and Advanced Commenting toolbars hold most of the tools you'll use for editing documents.

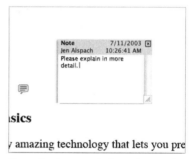

Figure 8.2 An expanded note is a good place to write detailed information about a specific area of a PDF document.

Figure 8.3 Text Edits lets you mark the document directly without having to open a note. Highlighting has been applied to this text.

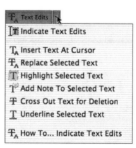

Figure 8.4 You can choose from a variety of Text Edit tools.

Figure 8.5 A sample stamp annotation. I chose the Approved stamp to indicate that this PDF is final.

Figure 8.6 The Highlight tool highlights areas of text

Figure 8.7 Drawing comments mark up this page.

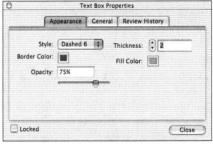

Figure 8.8 The Properties dialog box lets you change a variety of options.

- ◆ **Stamps** are graphics that can be applied to any page of a document (**Figure 8.5**). For example, you can use a stamp to show that the document has been reviewed and approved by you. You can also create custom stamps to indicate whatever you want.

- ◆ **Highlights** apply a certain effect to the selected text, including underline, strikethrough, and of course highlight (**Figure 8.6**). Most of these effects are also available under the Text Edits menu, but it's quicker to apply them directly from the Commenting toolbar.

- ◆ **Show** lets you see a reviewer's comments on the file. Choose Comments List from the Show pull-down menu and a Comments List pane appears at the bottom of your document. You can choose to sort the comments by a number of criteria, including by comment type, reviewer, or status. You can set your Commenting preferences by choosing Show > Commenting Preferences. For more on the Comments List, see "Viewing Comments" later in this chapter.

- ◆ The **Drawing** tools in the Advanced Commenting toolbar let you use graphic objects as comments. You can create rectangles, ovals, lines, polygons, and polygon lines to illustrate your point (**Figure 8.7**).

- ◆ **Text Box** comments in the Advanced Commenting toolbar allow you to add text in a box right in the document, like putting a sticky note right on the document. It doesn't collapse like a note does, and you can jazz up the box the note is in. You can access the Properties of the text box to change the font, box color, and other properties (**Figure 8.8**).

(continues on next page)

UNDERSTANDING THE TYPES OF COMMENTS

- The **Pencil** tool is a free-form drawing tool for custom marking (**Figure 8.9**).

- The **Pencil Eraser** tool lets you erase all or part of a shape made with the Pencil tool (**Figure 8.10**).

- **File attachments** are useful if you need to include more information than will fit in a note or text box, such as a source file or a file that contains updated or corrected information. You can change the icon for File Attachments in the Appearance tab of the File Attachment Properties dialog box (**Figure 8.11**). Sound attachments are files that contain recorded audio; they add a sound to a specific area of a PDF file. To change their properties, right-click/Control-click the Audio icon and choose Properties from the contextual menu to bring up the Sound Attachment Properties dialog box (**Figure 8.12**).

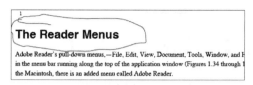

Figure 8.9 The Pencil tool lets you draw a free-form shape.

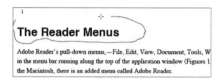

Figure 8.10 The Pencil Eraser tool lets you erase sections of the Pencil's drawn shape.

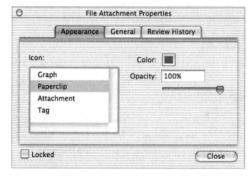

Figure 8.11 File Attachments lets you add a file or sound to a PDF document.

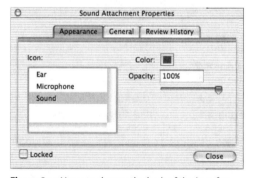

Figure 8.12 You can change the look of the icon for the Sound Attachment in the Properties dialog box.

Figure 8.13 Choose the Note tool from the Commenting toolbar.

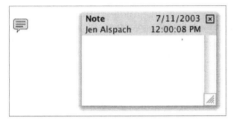

Figure 8.14 A note of default size is created when you just click.

Figure 8.15 Click and drag to create a note any size you'd like.

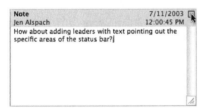

Figure 8.16 Close the note by clicking in the note's upper-right corner box.

Figure 8.17 The note icon remains visible in the document.

Creating and Editing Notes

Notes are the most basic form of comments. Think of them as sticky notes for your comments. You can use notes to keep track of changes or to indicate changes you'd like to see in text without actually making them. Because notes won't appear in a printed document, you can also use them to add information that's hidden from the public.

To create a note:

1. With a document open, choose the Note tool (**Figure 8.13**) from the Commenting toolbar.

2. Place the note by clicking the document page.

   A note of default size appears, with the name of the note's author and the date and time at the top (**Figure 8.14**).

   You can also drag with the Hand tool to create a different-size note box (**Figure 8.15**).

3. Type your note in the box.

4. If you want to close the note when you've finished entering text, click the close box in the top-right corner of the note (**Figure 8.16**).

   A note icon remains in the document at the spot you clicked to create the note (**Figure 8.17**).

(continues on next page)

CREATING AND EDITING NOTES

To edit an existing note:

1. Double-click the note icon to expand the note.

2. Click in the existing text to place the insertion point at that location (**Figure 8.18**).

3. Edit the text as desired, including cutting or copying text or pasting it from elsewhere.

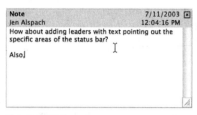

Figure 8.18 Place your mouse cursor where you want to insert the text.

✔ Tips

■ To set the font and size of the text in a note, choose Edit > Preferences > General (Ctrl-K/Command-K) to open the Preferences dialog box. Select Commenting in the list on the left side of the dialog box (**Figure 8.19**). Choose the font size from the pop-up menus, and set the opacity of the note boxes and the behavior of various types of comments.

■ You can edit or delete notes while the Hand tool is selected.

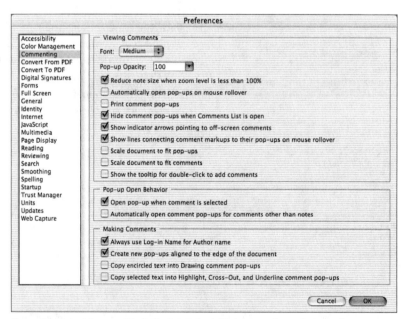

Figure 8.19 Select Commenting in the list on the left to change the preferences for comments.

CREATING AND EDITING NOTES

Reply
Set Status ▶
Mark with Checkmark

Close Pop-up Note
Reset Pop-up Note Location

Delete Comment

Show Comments List

Make Current Properties Default

Properties...

Figure 8.20 Right-click/Control-click to access the contextual menu for Properties.

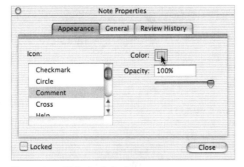

Figure 8.21 Click the Color button.

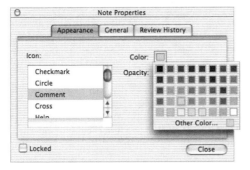

Figure 8.22 There are a bunch of preset colors to choose from.

Figure 8.23 Select Other Color to access your system's color picker.

To change the color of a note:

1. Right-click/Control-click the note icon and then choose Properties from the contextual menu (**Figure 8.20**).

   The Note Properties dialog box opens. Click the Appearance tab.

2. Click the Color button (**Figure 8.21**) to select a standard color or choose Other Color at the bottom (**Figure 8.22**).

   This brings up your system's color picker dialog box (**Figure 8.23**).

3. Choose a different color, and click OK to close the Color Picker.

4. Click Close in the Properties dialog box to change the note's color.

✔ Tips

■ You can change the note icon that appears in the document by selecting a new icon in the Appearance tab of the Note Properties dialog box.

■ To move a note, choose a different tool (I tend to choose the Hand tool), click on the note and drag it to a new location.

Using Text Edits

Text comments provide another method of adding and editing text in a document. More immediately visible than notes, text comments display the text directly in the document. These are the text edit options:

♦ **Indicate Text Edits** first selects the text that you want to apply an edit to. Drag the cursor across the text you want to select.

♦ **Insert Text at Cursor** inserts a caret at the selected point for you to insert text. The text will be inserted in a note box.

♦ **Replace Selected Text** will automatically cross out the selected text, insert a caret, and open an Inserted Text box (**Figure 8.24**).

♦ **Highlight Selected Text** essentially does the same as the Highlighter tool: Once you select the text and choose Highlight Selected Text, the text will be highlighted.

♦ **Add Note to Selected Text** automatically highlights the text and opens a Comment on Text box (**Figure 8.25**).

♦ **Cross Out Text for Deletion** does the same as the Cross-Out Text tool. It will cross out the selected text indicating deletion.

♦ **Underline Selected Text** does the same as the Underline Text tool.

To create a text edit:

1. Choose the Indicate Text Edits tool from the Commenting toolbar (**Figure 8.26**) by clicking the arrow next to Text Edits.

2. Drag to select the text that you want to edit (**Figure 8.27**).

Figure 8.24 Replace the selected text by adding new text in the box.

Figure 8.25 Add a note to the selected text.

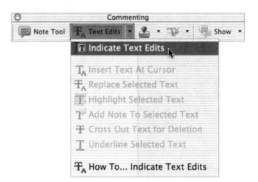

Figure 8.26 To start editing text, choose the Indicate Text Edits tool.

Figure 8.27 Drag over the text you want to make edits to.

USING TEXT EDITS

Figure 8.28 The caret marks where the new text should be inserted.

Figure 8.29 It's easy to replace text wherever you need to.

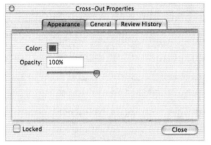

Figure 8.30 The Text Edit Properties dialog box lets you change options for the selected editing tool.

✔ Tip

■ The Appearance tab lets you change such properties as the color and opacity. The General tab lists the author, type of text edit, and date. The last tab lists the Review History and any changes to the comment. Although the Appearance tab options change depending on the type of edit that's selected, the latter two tabs are always the same.

3. Choose an edit function from the Text Edits menu.

   The chosen edit will affect the selected text.

To insert text:

1. With the Indicate Text Edits tool, select the area you where want to insert text.

2. Choose the Insert Text at Cursor tool. This will automatically insert a caret in the text and open a blue Inserted Text note box (**Figure 8.28**).

3. Type the text you want to insert in the note.

4. Close the note by clicking the close box in the top corner of the note box.

To replace text:

1. With the Indicate Text Edits tool, select the text you want to replace.

2. Choose the Replace Selected Text tool and the text you selected will automatically be crossed out, a caret will be inserted, and a blue Inserted Text note box will open (**Figure 8.29**).

3. Enter the text you want to be inserted into the note.

4. Close the note by clicking the close box in the top corner of the note box.

To change the properties of text edits:

1. Right-click/Control-click the text edit and then choose Properties from the contextual menu.

   The Properties dialog box for that edit type appears (**Figure 8.30**).

2. Change any of the options.

3. Click Close.

Using the Text Box Tool

Unlike many of the editing tools for text, the Text Box tool's comments remain visible in the document at all times. It's like adding a sticky note with your comments on it to a piece of paper. Double-click a text box to edit its properties.

To use the Text Box tool:

1. Select the Text Box tool in the Advanced Commenting toolbar.

2. Click and drag out a box the size of the comment you want to write.

3. Type your comment (**Figure 8.31**).

To change the properties of a text box:

1. Right-click/Control-click the text box to activate the contextual menu.

2. Choose Properties.

3. In the Text Box Properties dialog box (**Figure 8.32**), make your changes.

   You can change the line style, border color, opacity, thickness (in pixels), and fill color of the box. As you change the properties, the box simultaneously changes in the document.

4. Click the Close button.

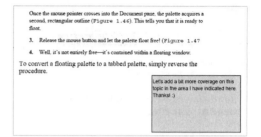

Figure 8.31 Type your comment at the blinking cursor.

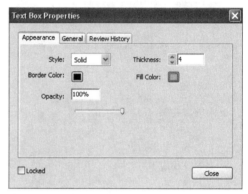

Figure 8.32 Change settings in the Text Box Properties dialog box.

Figure 8.33 Choose the Sound Attachment tool from the pop-up menu under the File Attachment tool in the Advanced Commenting toolbar.

Figure 8.34 Choose or record a sound in the Record Sound dialog box.

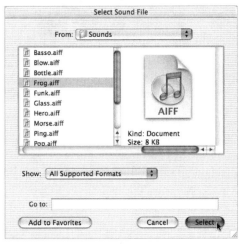

Figure 8.35 Choose a sound on your system.

Using Audio Attachments

To add spoken commentary (or a musical interlude, if the document calls for it) to a PDF document, use an audio attachment. If your computer has a microphone or you have sounds on your system already, you can easily add sound to a PDF.

To attach a sound to a document:

1. Choose the Sound Attachment tool from the Advanced Commenting toolbar (**Figure 8.33**).

2. Place the sound attachment by clicking the document page.
   The Record Sound dialog box appears (**Figure 8.34**).

3. Click the Choose button to bring up the Select Sound File dialog box and access the sounds on your computer, or click Record to record your own sound and attach it.

4. Navigate to the sound that you want to use and click the Select button (**Figure 8.35**). You can choose from WAV and AIFF sound attachments.

(continues on next page)

5. To hear the sound, click the Play button, then click the Close button.

The Sound Attachment Properties dialog box opens automatically, in case you want to make any changes (**Figure 8.36**). An icon appears on the page where your attachment was placed (**Figure 8.37**). Click the sound attachment icon to play the sound.

✔ Tips

■ To record sounds, click the Record button, speak into your computer's microphone, then click the Stop button. This adds a more personal touch to your comments on the PDF file.

■ Be aware that attaching even a short sound can greatly increase the size of your PDF file, so make sure it's worth the extra bytes.

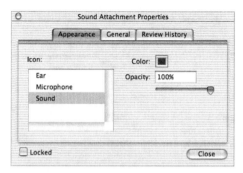

Figure 8.36 Use the Sound Attachment Properties dialog box to make any changes.

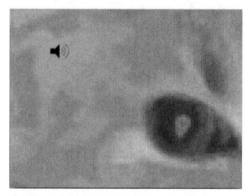

Figure 8.37 A speaker icon appears where you attached your sound.

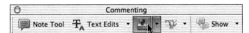

Figure 8.38 To stamp a document, choose the Stamp tool from the toolbar.

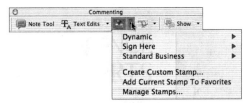

Figure 8.39 Choose a stamp from the categories under the Stamp tool.

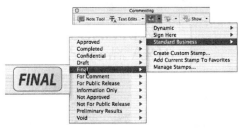

Figure 8.40 You see a preview of each stamp in the category submenus.

Stamping PDFs

My favorite commenting feature is the Stamp tool, which allows you to place stamps anywhere in a document. You can stamp a document as Confidential, Top Secret, as a Working Draft, or For Your Eyes Only. You can even add custom stamps; any graphic file saved as a PDF can be placed as a custom stamp. Several stamp categories are built in:

◆ **Dynamic** stamps include information on when and by whom the stamp was applied.

◆ **Sign Here** stamp choices are Rejected, Accepted, Initial Here, Sign Here, and Witness.

◆ **Standard Business** stamps include Approved, Completed, Confidential, Draft, Final, Not Approved, Not for Public Release, and Void.

To add a stamp to a document:

1. Open the document open that you want to stamp, and choose the Stamp tool from the Commenting toolbar (**Figure 8.38**).

2. From the pop-up menu under the Stamp tool, choose a category submenu and select the stamp you want to use (**Figure 8.39**).

   Next to the name, you can see a preview of the stamp you've chosen (**Figure 8.40**).

   (continues on next page)

3. Click in the document or drag over an area that matches the size of the stamp you chose (you can always resize it later).

A stamp appears (**Figure 8.41**).

4. Right-click/Control-click the stamp and select Properties from the contextual menu.

The Stamp Properties dialog box appears (**Figure 8.42**).

5. Change any of the stamp's properties (color and opacity of the note attached with the stamp), then click OK.

✔ Tip

■ If you click with the Stamp tool, you'll place the last stamp you selected. You can always change the stamp by choosing another from the menu.

To remove a stamp from a document:

◆ Click the stamp to select it and then press Backspace/Delete.

or

Right-click/Control-click the stamp and then choose Delete from the contextual menu.

Figure 8.41 Your stamp appears on your document, at any size you drag it to be.

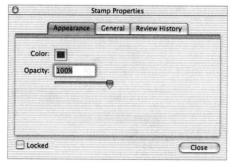

Figure 8.42 The Stamp Properties dialog box lets you change some options for the stamp.

Figure 8.43 Here's the Illustrator artwork I've created to use as a custom stamp within Acrobat.

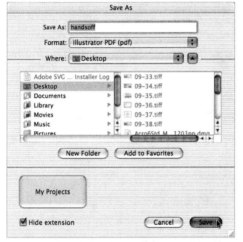

Figure 8.44 When I save the file, I give it a name—Handsoff—that tells me what to look for within Acrobat.

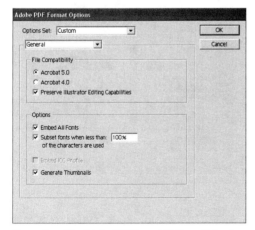

Figure 8.45 The Adobe PDF Format Options dialog box lets you choose your PDF settings.

Creating Custom Stamps

You can use any graphic program that can save a file as PDF to create custom stamps for Acrobat. You'll get better results, however, if you create the graphic in a vector-based program such as Illustrator, because you'll be able to resize the stamp and keep the clean vector lines, rather than getting pixilated edges. Because Acrobat treats PDF documents as containers for stamps, you can export an Illustrator document as a PDF page and use that "page" as a stamp. Acrobat knows enough to discard the white space around the graphic, so only the content area of the page will become the new stamp.

To create a custom stamp in Illustrator and Acrobat:

1. In Illustrator, create the artwork you want to use as a stamp (**Figure 8.43**).

2. Choose Save As from the File menu. The Save As dialog box appears (**Figure 8.44**).

3. Choose Acrobat PDF from the Format pop-up menu. This brings up the Adobe PDF Format Options dialog box (**Figure 8.45**). Choose your settings and click OK.

4. In the Save As dialog box, choose a save location and click OK to save your artwork as a PDF.

(continues on next page)

CREATING CUSTOM STAMPS

5. In Acrobat, choose Create Custom Stamp from the Stamp tool pop-up menu (**Figure 8.46**). This brings up the Create Stamp dialog box (**Figure 8.47**).

6. Click the Select button to bring up the Select dialog box (**Figure 8.48**).

7. Enter the name of the file, or click the Browse button to bring up the Open dialog box.

8. Navigate to the file and click the Select button (**Figure 9.49**). This takes you back to the Select dialog box, now displaying the stamp and the location. Click the OK button to return to the Create Stamp dialog box.

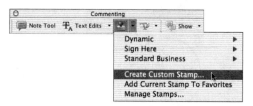

Figure 8.46 Choose Create Custom Stamp from the Stamp tool's pop-up menu.

Figure 8.47 The Create Stamp dialog box lets you find the stamp and name it.

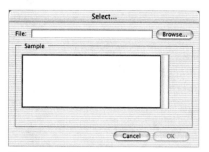

Figure 8.48 Click the Browse button to find your stamp.

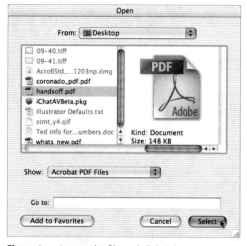

Figure 8.49 Locate the file and click Select.

Figure 8.50 The stamp you created will show as a small icon.

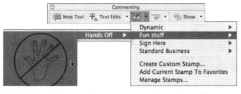

Figure 8.51 Choose the new stamp from the submenu for the category you specified.

Figure 8.52 Place the new stamp and drag it out to the size you'd like.

Figure 8.53 Add or delete stamps in the Manage Stamps dialog box.

9. You'll now see the stamp in the Create Stamp dialog box. Enter a category and a name for the new stamp, then click OK (**Figure 8.50**).

10. Choose the new stamp from the Stamp tool menu (**Figure 8.51**).

11. Drag out your new stamp to the size you'd like (**Figure 8.52**).

✔ Tip

■ To remove any custom stamps, choose Manage Stamps from the Stamp menu. In the Manage Stamps dialog box (**Figure 8.53**), you can add or delete any stamps you've created, add categories for organizing your stamps, and change your stamps' categories. You can also add your stamp to your favorite stamps.

Creating a File Attachment

You can attach any type of file to a PDF document using the Advanced Commenting toolbar. It could be an image, a spreadsheet, or another PDF file. In some cases, you might even want to attach the non-PDF source file to the PDF document.

To attach a file to a document:

1. With a document open, choose the File Attachment tool from the Advanced Commenting toolbar (**Figure 8.54**).

2. Click in the PDF document where you'd like to attach the file.

   The Select File to Attach dialog box appears (**Figure 8.55**).

3. Navigate to the file you want to attach, and click Select.

   The File Attachment Properties dialog box appears (**Figure 8.56**).

4. In the Appearance tab, select the icon you would like to use, and its opacity and color.

5. If you like, type a description and other information in the General tab (**Figure 8.57**).

6. Click Close.

   The file is attached to the document. When you click the icon, the attached file will open.

✔ Tip

■ When you attach a file to a PDF document, you are embedding that file within the document. This means that the PDF file contains the attached file, dramatically increasing its size. If the file you're attaching is a large one, turn it into a PDF and add those pages to the existing PDF, then link to those pages from the same location where you'd have placed the file-attachment annotation. For information on links, see Chapter 7.

Figure 8.54 Choose the Attach File tool.

Figure 8.55 The Select File to Attach dialog box comes up so you can choose the right file.

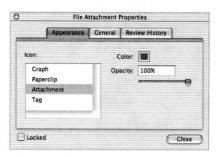

Figure 8.56 Choose a different icon in the File Attachment Properties dialog box.

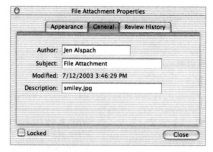

Figure 8.57 Enter any description you'd like in the General tab.

Figure 8.58 From the Advanced Commenting toolbar, select the tool you want to draw with.

Figure 8.59 The Pencil and Pencil Eraser tools have their own slot, and all the shape tools live under the Rectangle tool.

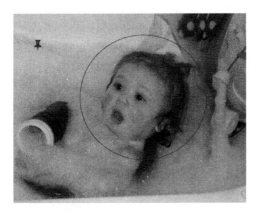

Figure 8.60 Drag in the document page to draw with a shape tool.

Editing with the Drawing Tools

Use the drawing tools as you would use a pencil or pen, to show the areas you want to edit and to enhance your PDF page. The drawing tools are Rectangle, Oval, Line, Polygon, Polygon Line, Pencil, and Pencil Eraser.

To mark up a page with the drawing tools:

1. Select the tool you want to use from the Advanced Commenting toolbar (**Figure 8.58**).

   The drawing tools share two slots in the toolbar. The Pencil and Pencil Eraser tools have their own space. The other drawing tools are housed under the Rectangle tool (**Figure 8.59**).

2. Click or drag in the document page to draw with the tool you've selected (**Figure 8.60**).

✔ Tip

- You can change the size of the shape you created by selecting the shape with the Hand tool. Adjustment handles appear on the shape, and you can drag them out (to make larger or wider) or in (to make smaller or thinner). As you drag the box corner, hold the Shift key to preserve the proportions of the shape.

To use the Pencil tool:

1. Select the Pencil tool from the Advanced Commenting toolbar (**Figure 8.61**).

2. Drag out a free-form shape with the Pencil tool (**Figure 8.62**). A box appears around the shape.

3. Click with the Hand tool to deselect the shape.

To use the Pencil Eraser tool:

1. Select the Pencil Eraser tool from the Advanced Commenting toolbar.

2. Click the shape to erase small sections of the path. You can also just drag the tool across an area you want to delete (**Figure 8.63**).

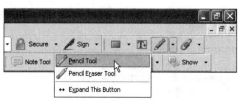

Figure 8.61 Select the Pencil tool from the Advanced Commenting toolbar.

Figure 8.62 Drag out the free-form shape.

Figure 8.63 Drag or click with the Pencil Eraser tool to remove sections of the free-form path.

Figure 8.64 Choose Properties from the contextual menu.

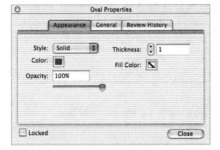

Figure 8.65 The Properties for the selected tool appears.

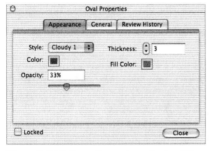

Figure 8.66 Select a line style and color, fill color, opacity, and line thickness.

Figure 8.67 The shape changes to the Cloudy 1 line style. Pretty cute!

To change the line weight and color:

1. With the Hand tool, right-click/Control-click the edge of the line you have drawn.

2. Choose Properties from the contextual menu (**Figure 8.64**).

   The Properties dialog box for the selected shape appears (**Figure 8.65**).

3. In the Thickness field, type a new value or click the up and down arrows to change the thickness.

4. Choose a line type from the Style pop-up menu.

   I'm choosing Cloudy 1 for this example.

5. Make selections for the outline color, fill color, and opacity, if desired (**Figure 8.66**). The changes take effect immediately (**Figure 8.67**).

6. Click Close in the Properties dialog box.

✔ Tips

■ With the Rectangle, Polygon, and Oval tools, you can choose different border and fill colors.

■ In the General tab of the Properties dialog box, you can add a note to the drawing.

■ Hold down the Shift key to constrain your lines to 45-degree angles, your ellipses to circles, and your rectangles to squares. The Shift key has no effect on the Pencil tool.

EDITING WITH THE DRAWING TOOLS

Marking up Text with Highlighting Tools

One set of Acrobat's commenting tools can be used to mark up words directly, rather than the page near the text. These tools are grouped under the Highlighter tool on the Commenting toolbar, and include the Underline and Cross-out tools (**Figure 8.68**). Click the arrow next to the Highlighter tool to access the other tools.

To mark up text directly:

1. In the Commenting toolbar, choose the Highlighting tool you want to use.

2. Click a single word to apply the effect to the word.

   or

   Drag the tool across the text you want to mark.

   The effect is applied to the text (**Figure 8.69**).

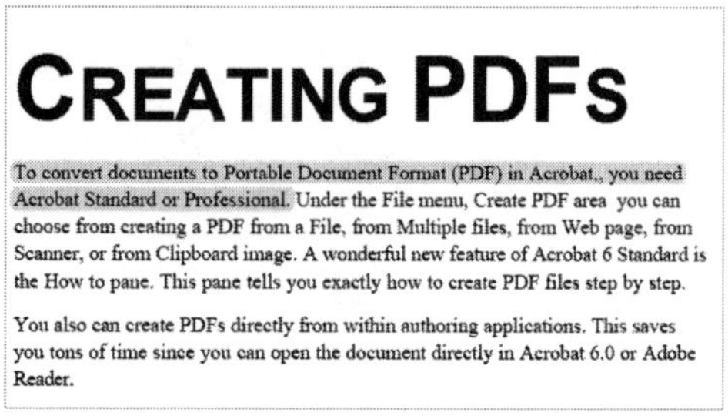

To change highlight color:

1. With the Hand tool selected, right-click/Control-click the highlighted text to activate the contextual menu.

2. Choose Properties from the menu.
   The Properties dialog box for the selected highlight appears.

3. Click the Color swatch, and choose a preset color, or choose Other Color to activate your system's color picker.

4. Click Close to apply the color to the highlight, cross-out line, or underline.

✔ Tips

■ These tools select whole words; they can't act on a single character or part of a word.

■ As with the other commenting tools, you can add a note to a highlight in the General tab of the Properties dialog box.

Figure 8.68 The Cross-Out and Underline tools are listed under the Highlight tool.

CREATING PDFS

To convert documents to Portable Document Format (PDF) in Acrobat,, you need Acrobat Standard or Professional. Under the File menu, Create PDF area you can choose from creating a PDF from a File, from Multiple files, from Web page, from Scanner, or from Clipboard image. A wonderful new feature of Acrobat 6 Standard is the How to pane. This pane tells you exactly how to create PDF files step by step.

You also can create PDFs directly from within authoring applications. This saves you tons of time since you can open the document directly in Acrobat 6.0 or Adobe Reader.

Figure 8.69 The effect is applied to the text.

MARKING UP TEXT WITH HIGHLIGHTING TOOLS

Figure 8.70 Select the TouchUp Text tool from the Advanced Editing toolbar.

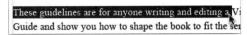

Figure 8.71 Drag to select the text you want to touch up.

Editing Text

Another way to edit a document is to actually change the text, not just comment on it. You can change any text in Acrobat with the TouchUp Text tool in the Advanced Editing toolbar. Unlike the Select Text tool, TouchUp Text enables you to change the text.

To use the TouchUp Text tool:

1. Select the TouchUp Text tool in the Advanced Editing toolbar (**Figure 8.70**).

2. Click any text in the PDF document. A box appears around the line of text.

3. Select text within the box by dragging across it (**Figure 8.71**).

4. Replace the selected text by typing, or delete it by pressing the Backspace/ Delete key.

✔ Tip

■ Double-clicking text selects one word at a time; clicking three times selects an entire row of text.

EDITING TEXT

You can also use the TouchUp Text tool to adjust the typographical attributes of a line of text.

To edit text attributes:

1. Select the TouchUp Text tool in the Advanced Commenting toolbar.

2. Click anywhere within the line of text you want to change.

   A box appears around the line.

3. Right-click/Control-click the text, then choose Properties from the contextual menu to access the TouchUp Properties dialog box (**Figure 8.72**).

   You can use this dialog box to apply the following options to selected text:

   ▲ **Font** lists all fonts installed in your system or embedded in the PDF.

   ▲ **Font Size** lets you choose text size from 6-point to 72-point type.

   ▲ **Character Spacing** lets you adjust the spacing between two or more characters.

   ▲ **Word Spacing** lets you adjust the spacing between two or more words.

   ▲ **Horizontal Scale** sets the ratio between the width and the height of the type.

   ▲ **Embed Font** lets you specify whether to embed the font in the PDF.

   ▲ **Fill Color** and **Stroke Color** let you change the color of selected text.

   ▲ **Stroke Width** lets you enter a stroke weight in points for the selected text. In other words, you choose the weight of the line around each individual letter.

   ▲ **Baseline Offset** sets the text's vertical offset from the baseline (also known as superscript or subscript style).

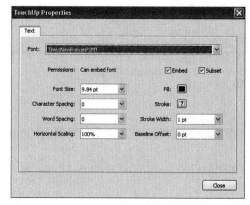

Figure 8.72 Use the TouchUp Properties dialog box to change text attributes.

Figure 8.73 The Comments List in the bottom half of your document screen lists all comments in a document.

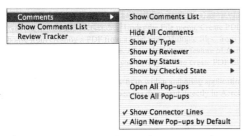

Figure 8.74 There are various options you can choose when viewing comments.

Figure 8.75 Show By Type hides all but the type of comment you choose.

Figure 8.76 Show By Status filters comments according to how they've been acted on.

Viewing Comments

You can view your comments on the page or at the bottom of the screen, or hide them entirely. Simply choose View > Comments > Show Comments List, or choose Show Comments List under the Review & Comment menu. When the Comments List is visible on the bottom half of your screen (**Figure 8.73**), you can hide it again by choosing View > Comments > Hide Comments List.

These are the other viewing options in the Commenting toolbar's Show menu (**Figure 8.74**):

◆ **Hide All Comments** hides all comments added to the PDF file.

◆ **Show by Type** lets you choose whether to view all comments or a single type of comment (**Figure 8.75**).

◆ **Show by Reviewer** lets you filter comments according to who wrote them.

◆ **Show by Status** lets you see comments that have been accepted, rejected, cancelled, completed or that have no status (**Figure 8.76**). For more on comment status, see Chapter 9.

◆ **Show by Checked State** lists comments according to whether they've been checked.

◆ **Open All Pop-ups** opens up all notes and pop-up comments.

◆ **Close All Pop-ups** closes all notes and pop-up comments.

◆ **Show Connecter Lines** shows the lines that connect a comment to a note.

(continues on next page)

VIEWING COMMENTS

◆ **Align New Pop-ups by Default** aligns all notes' pop-up windows vertically along one of the margins.

In the Comments List, there are more menus full of commands for working with your comments:

◆ **Expand all elements in the panel** lets you expand and see all comments in the Comments pane and the information such as author, type of comment, date, and the comment.

◆ **Collapse all elements in the panel** collapses the comments to just the page that a comment is on.

◆ **Go to the next comment** takes you to the next consecutive comment.

◆ **Go to the previous comment** goes back to the previous comment.

◆ **Reply to the selected comment** lets you reply to someone's comment. You choose the comment first, then click the Reply button. A new line will appear in the Comments List for you to enter your reply (**Figure 8.77**).

◆ **Delete the selected comment** removes the comment you selected.

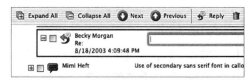

Figure 8.77 Use the Reply button to enter a reaction to someone's comment.

♦ **Set the comment status** shows whether the comment was accepted, rejected, cancelled, or completed. Select the comment first, then choose one of the status options. The status option shows up in a line below the comment.

♦ **Checkmark** marks the selected comment; useful for keeping track of which comments you've looked at.

♦ **Show** lets you filter the various comment types as explained above.

♦ **Sort By** lets you change the order in which comments are listed (by type, page, author, color, checkmark status, or status by person).

♦ **Search** lets you search the comments for a specific word or phrase.

♦ **Print Comments** allows you to print a summary of comments, create a PDF, and several more options, which are covered in "Summarizing Comments," later in this chapter.

♦ **Options** holds a menu of commands for use on comments: Summarize Comments, Import Comments, Export Selected Comments, Open Review Tracker, and Scan for Comments. For more on summarizing see the tasks later in this chapter. For more on reviewing, see Chapter 9.

VIEWING COMMENTS

Deleting Comments

You can delete comments at any time, using the Hand, Selection, or any comment tool.

To delete a comment:

1. Using any tool, click the comment you want to get rid of to select it.

   The mouse pointer changes to an arrow pointer when it's over an existing comment.

2. Press Backspace/Delete.

   or

   Choose Edit > Clear.

   or

   Right-click/Control-click the comment and then choose Delete from the contextual menu (**Figure 8.78**).

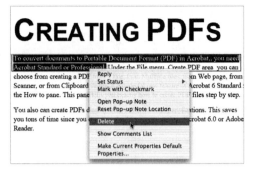

Figure 8.78 Choose the appropriate command from the contextual menu and the comment will be deleted.

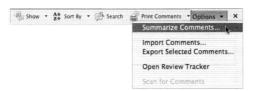

Figure 8.79 Choose Summarize Comments from the Options menu.

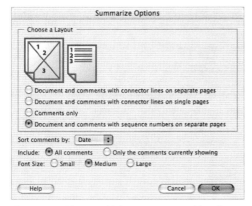

Figure 8.80 Choose which comments to add to the summary, and how they'll be displayed.

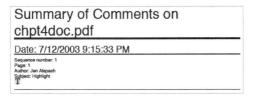

Figure 8.81 The new document appears with all of the comments listed.

Summarizing Comments

Acrobat provides a method for summarizing all the comments in a document quickly. This feature actually creates a new PDF file with the comments listed and completely labeled, including their type, author, and date. The comments are viewed in the bottom half of the document window. The Comments List toolbar that lets you access the commenting menu items quickly.

To create a summary of the comments in a document:

1. Choose Summarize Comments from the Options menu in the Comments List (**Figure 8.79**).

   The Summarize Options dialog box appears (**Figure 8.80**).

2. Choose how to sort comments: by author, date, page, or type of annotation.

   You can also choose how the summary document shows comments: with or without the original document, with or without connector lines, and on single pages or on separate pages. As you select each radio button, the icon in the dialog box changes to show a representation of that choice. Other options include summarizing only currently shown comments and choosing a font size for the summary.

   Acrobat will churn a bit if you have a large number of comments. Then a new document appears, with all comments listed (**Figure 8.81**).

After you've viewed the comments, you can save the PDF file, print it, or close it without saving it.

(continues on next page)

SUMMARIZING COMMENTS

✔ Tips

- I suggest that you select "Document and comments with connector lines on single pages," so you can see what the comments refer to. It may be a larger file, but it's easier to understand.

- Text that has been marked up with the Highlight tools, Drawing tools, and Pencil tools also appear in the summary, along with notes of any attached files or sounds.

REVIEWING

Adobe has continued to advance the paper-less workflow, making life easier for far-flung groups working on a single document. Now in Acrobat 6.0, you have several choices for initiating a review of PDF documents. Not only can you send your PDF to colleagues and ask them to export their comments and send them back, you can start an email-based review or a browser-based review that people access on the Web. Furthermore, you can track the reviews using Acrobat's Review tracker.

Setting Up Document Review

Sending PDF files to other people for review is a great way to connect people in different locations who work on the same project. You can email the PDF to someone for review, or (in Windows) post the PDF to a Web page for review.

To email a PDF document for review:

1. Open the document you want to send for review.

2. In the Tasks toolbar, choose Review & Comment > Send by Email for Review. If the Tasks toolbar isn't showing, choose View > Toolbars > Tasks.

3. This brings up a dialog box asking for the email address from which you'll be initiating the review (**Figure 9.1**). Enter your email address and press OK.

   Your email program will launch or come to the front if it is already running. The active PDF file is automatically attached to a new email.

4. Type the email addresses of the people you want to send to (**Figure 9.2**).

   Acrobat automatically generates reviewing instructions in the body of the email (**Figure 9.3**), telling reviewers how to add their comments to the PDF. You can change this standard text or add your own before you send the email.

5. Click the Send button.

   When reviewers open the file, they get a message letting them know that the file is part of an email-based review (**Figure 9.4**).

Figure 9.1 Acrobat needs to know where you're emailing from.

Figure 9.2 Enter recipients' email addresses in the text fields.

Figure 9.3 Instructions are automatically entered in the body of the email.

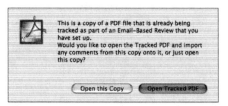

Figure 9.4 The reviewer gets a message that he or she is part of an email-based review.

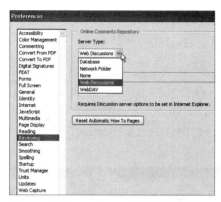

Figure 9.5 Choose a Server type for the Web-based review.

Figure 9.6 Click Reset Automatic How To Pages to show the appropriate topics for your reviewers.

To set up a Web-based review (Windows only):

1. First you must save the PDF file on a server that others can access on the Web.

2. Choose Edit > Preferences. This opens the Preferences window.

3. Choose Reviewing from the list on the left.

4. Choose your server type from the drop-down menu (**Figure 9.5**).

   Make sure you get the specifics for the server settings from your system administrator.

5. Click Reset Automatic How To Pages.

   This will ensure that the How To window shows the correct Reviewing and Commenting topics for your reviewers (**Figure 9.6**): Start a Review, Participate in a Review, and Adding Comments.

6. Click OK to close the Preferences window.

SETTING UP DOCUMENT REVIEW

To upload a PDF document for Web discussion (Windows only):

1. Open the document you want to upload for review.

2. In the Tasks toolbar choose Review & Comment > Upload for Browser-Based Review (**Figure 9.7**).

   The Upload for Review dialog box opens (**Figure 9.8**).

3. Choose a save location for the PDF file you want to upload and then click Upload to upload the file, and open the Start Browser-Based Review dialog box (**Figure 9.9**).

4. Enter the emails of the reviewers in the To, Cc, and Bcc fields, as appropriate.

   Your email program will launch or come to the front if it is already running. The currently active PDF file is automatically attached to a new email. The body of the email contains reviewing instructions automatically entered by Acrobat, which you can change or add to, if you like.

5. Click the Send button to start the review.

Figure 9.7 To upload a PDF, choose Upload for Browser-Based Review under Review & Comment in the Tasks toolbar.

Figure 9.8 Choose the location and click Upload.

Figure 9.9 The dialog box lets you start the review process.

Figure 9.10 Choose Invite More Reviewers from the Review & Comment menu.

Figure 9.11 You can also invite more reviewers from the Review & Comment pane under the Manage menu.

Inviting Additional Reviews

Once you get a project going, you'll undoubtedly want your peers and colleagues to review and comment on it. If a whole group of people are looking at the PDF and commenting on it, you'll need to manage the reviewers and comments. Acrobat provides you with a way to invite and manage reviews.

To invite review of a PDF:

1. With the PDF open, choose Invite More Reviewers from the Review & Comment menu (**Figure 9.10**).

   or

   Select the file from the Review & Comment pane on the left side of the screen (if it isn't showing, choose View > Review Tracker), and choose Invite more Reviewers from the Manage menu (**Figure 9.11**).

   Your email program will launch or come to the front if it is already running. The currently active PDF file is automatically attached to a new email. Enter the email addresses of the people you want to invite.

2. Change the default body text as necessary and click Send.

To send your reviewers a reminder (Windows only):

1. Select the PDF file in the Review and Comment pane and choose Send Review Reminder.

   This will open your email program.

2. Enter the names of the reviewers you want to email.

3. Click the Send button. The reminder email is sent to the reviewers.

Online Reviewing

When you've been invited to review a PDF document by email, just opening the attachment begins the review process. Add your comments to the PDF file and upload them for other reviewers to see, or save the file to your computer for offline reviewing. You can download other reviewers' comments, as well.

To start reviewing a PDF in a Web browser:

1. Once you receive the email inviting you to participate, open the attached file. This will launch your Web browser, showing the file from the server.

2. Using the tools in the Commenting and Advanced Commenting toolbar, add your comments to the PDF file online in the Web browser. See Chapter 8 for information on working with the commenting tools.

   You can also save a copy to work offline.

To send and receive comments:

1. Enter your comments directly in the PDF file.

2. When you're ready to send, choose Review & Comment > Send and Receive Comments (**Figure 9.12**).

   The comments from other reviewers are now visible and your comments have been sent for other reviewers to see (**Figure 9.13**).

Figure 9.12 One menu item lets you send and receive comments simultaneously.

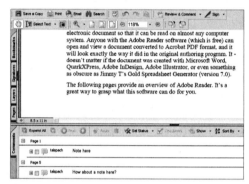

Figure 9.13 You'll see other reviewers' comments appear in the Comments List.

Figure 9.14 Using the Hand tool, right-click/Control-click the note and choose Reply.

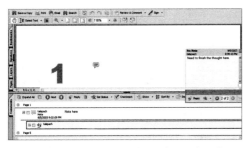

Figure 9.15 Enter your text in the reply note box that appears in both the Comments List and on the document.

Figure 9.16 Check the number of replies to the original note. There are three replies to the note above, and the second one is displayed.

To comment on another reviewer's comment:

1. With the Hand tool, right-click/Control-click the note and choose Reply from the toolbar that appears (**Figure 9.14**). This opens a new note box both in the Document pane and in the Comments List, headed "Re:Note," where you can enter your reply (**Figure 9.15**).

2. Enter your reply or replies to the note. You'll notice that in the Reply box, there's more than one reply (**Figure 9.16**). You can view them one at a time by clicking the Next Comment arrow, or click the View All button on the toolbar to see all replies.

Changing Status of a Comment

As you review documents, you can make it clear which comments were read by changing their status to Accepted, Rejected, Cancelled, or Completed. This is particularly helpful when you want to show or hide certain comments—after changing the status of a bunch of comments, you can sort by status to show only Accepted ones, for example.

To change the status of a comment:

1. In the document that you're reviewing, choose View > Comments > Show Comments List.

   The Comments List opens.

2. Select the comment you want to change by clicking it in the Comments List (**Figure 9.17**).

3. Choose an option from the Set Status menu in the Commenting toolbar (**Figure 9.18**).

   The comment's status is shown below it (**Figure 9.19**).

Figure 9.17 Select the comments whose status you want to change.

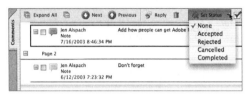

Figure 9.18 Choose a Set Status option.

Figure 9.19 The comment's status—in this case, Completed—appears below and to the right of the comment.

Figure 9.20 Remove a comment by clicking the trashcan icon with the comment selected.

Deleting Comments

To clean up a document, you may want to delete some of the comments that have been added by reviewers, for example the comments that were rejected or cancelled.

To delete a comment:

1. In the document that you're reviewing, choose View > Comments > Show Comments List.

2. Click the comment that you want to delete in the Comments pane.

3. Click the trashcan icon in the Comments pane toolbar (**Figure 9.20**).

   or

   Press the Delete/Backspace key.

✔ Tip

■ You can get the comment back if you Undo (Ctrl-Z/Command-Z) right after you delete it, or by reverting to the last saved version of the document (File > Revert).

Exporting and Importing Comments

Whether you're directly participating in a review or not, you can import and read others' comments and export your own comments. When you import or export comments, you actually create an FDF file (form data format), which contains only the comments and not the whole file. You can open an FDF file with any text editor, but the best way to apply comments to the document is to have the original or a copy of the PDF file that is being commented on. Import the comments to that original PDF and the comments will line up in the correct locations.

To export comments:

1. In the PDF file with your comments, choose Document > Export Comments. You can do this as a reviewer, an offline reviewer, or as the initiator of the review so everyone can see your comments.

2. In the Export Comments dialog box that appears, choose Acrobat FDF Files or Acrobat XFDF Files from the Save as Type or Select (Macintosh) menu (**Figure 9.21**).

3. Choose a save location for the exported file on your computer, and enter a name for the file (**Figure 9.22**).

4. Click Save. This will create the FDF file with only the comments and save it on your computer. You can then email your comments to other reviewers, and they'll appear in the same place in the original PDF when they're imported.

To export selected comments:

1. In the Comments pane, select the comments to be exported (**Figure 9.23**). Select one comment by clicking it; select multiple comments by Ctrl/Command-clicking.

Figure 9.21 Choose the Acrobat FDF or Acrobat XFDF file type.

Figure 9.22 Choose a name and location for the exported file.

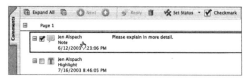

Figure 9.23 Select the comments you want to export.

Using the Review Tracker

The Review Tracker keeps track of all the
PDF documents you've sent or received for
email, browser, and offline reviews. Use it to
send a reminder, invite more reviewers,
remove reviewed files, open the PDF file that
the review is based on. The Manage option
also lets you email all reviewers, send a
reminder, and go back online when you've
been reviewing offline.

To work with Review Tracker:

1. Choose Review & Comment > Track
   Reviews.
   or
   Choose Open Review Tracker from the
   Options menu in the Comments List.
   or
   Choose View > Review Tracker (**Figure
   9.28**).
   This opens the Review & Comment pane
   to the right of the document (**Figure 9.29**).

2. Choose the Review you want to alter.

3. You can choose to open the PDF, remove
   the PDF, or one of the Manage options.

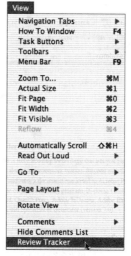

Figure 9.28 Choose View >
Review Tracker to see the
Review & Comment pane.

Figure 9.29 The Review & Comment
pane lets you manage your reviews.

USING THE REVIEW TRACKER

10

PAPER CAPTURE

Wouldn't it be nice to convert all your paper-based documents to PDF files? Then you could archive those documents electronically and distribute them by email or CD-ROM. Acrobat includes a plug-in that helps you do just this.

Acrobat lets you scan in documents that contain images, text, columns, and more, while retaining links, images, colors, fonts, and other elements.

Scanning a Document into Acrobat

To turn a paper document into a PDF, you first have to create an image of it in your computer. The most direct way is by scanning the document. You can have Acrobat control the scanning process by using the Import command.

Using scanning software

In general, when you install the software that came with your scanner, the installation program will find scanner-capable programs on your computer and install the software that operates the scanner (usually, in the form of a plug-in) in each of those programs.

Scanning images and text

When you are scanning documents, you must keep in mind that the higher the quality of the scan, the larger the resulting image file will be. The trick is getting the best scan for your purposes without creating a file that's bigger than you need, which takes up space on your hard disk and is slow to manipulate.

Before starting to scan, think carefully about two parameters in your scanning software: color mode and resolution. For the color-mode setting, you'll normally choose grayscale or color. If the document you're scanning was printed in full color, use color (**Figure 10.1**). If your document was printed in black ink, choose the grayscale option. Scan color images in grayscale mode if you want to keep down the file size or if the PDF will be printed only on ordinary laser printers.

Figure 10.1 Choose the color mode that matches your needs.

Figure 10.2 You can create a PDF from a Scanner.

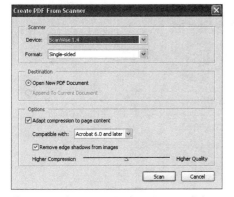

Figure 10.3 The Create PDF from Scanner dialog box appears for you to choose your scanner.

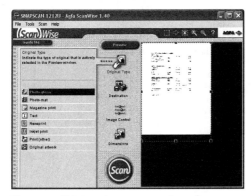

Figure 10.4 This launches your scanning software.

Resolution is the fineness of detail in the scan, measured in dots per inch (dpi). Choose a resolution based on the content of the document and how you plan to use the PDF. If the document consists only of images that people will read onscreen, a resolution of around 75 dpi is fine. If your document contains text, and you intend to convert the scan into searchable text (*capture* it, in Acrobat jargon), you need to scan at a much higher resolution—say, 300 dpi. Line art requires a resolution of approximately 600 dpi.

To scan an image to be captured:

1. Place the document to be scanned face-down on the scanner.

2. Choose File > Create PDF > From Scanner (**Figure 10.2**), or click the Create PDF button and choose From Scanner from the pop-up menu.

   The Create PDF from Scanner dialog box appears (**Figure 10.3**).

3. From the Device pop-up menu, choose your scanner.

4. Choose Single-Sided or Double-Sided from the Format menu, depending on the nature of your original.

5. In the Destination section, specify whether you want to create a new PDF from the scanned material or add the material to the currently active PDF. You can also choose several other options (adapt compression to page content, compatibility versions, remove edge shadows from images, and set higher compression or higher quality).

6. Click Scan.

   Your scanner's software launches (**Figure 10.4**).

(continues on next page)

SCANNING A DOCUMENT INTO ACROBAT

7. Enter your settings for type of image or color mode, destination (where to save the file), and resolution.

8. Click the Scan button to start the scan into Acrobat. You'll see the progress of the scan (**Figure 10.5**).

9. If you are scanning more documents, click the Next button in the Acrobat Scan Plug-In dialog box (**Figure 10.6**) and keep scanning.

10. Click the Done button when you finish scanning documents.

   Acrobat converts the image to an untitled PDF document (**Figure 10.7**).

11. Save and name the new PDF file.

✔ Tips

■ You can always rotate a scanned page in Acrobat by choosing Document > Pages > Rotate Pages (Ctrl+Shift+R/Command+ Shift+R). You can rotate specific pages or all pages.

■ If the scan has extra space around it, choose Document > Pages > Crop Pages (Ctrl+Shift+T/Command+Shift+T). This command lets you crop one or all pages.

Figure 10.5 Watch the progress of your scan.

Figure 10.6 Click Next to scan another document.

Week #9 Workout: Cardio with weights:			
Day #1: Legs:			
Squat w/ Side Raise		25reps	3sets
Traveling Lunges	8lbs		6sets
(Varying type)			
Side Lunges	8lbs		4sets
Day #2: Chest and Back:			
Pectoral Fly	5-8lbs	25reps	4sets
Push Ups		25reps	4sets
Lat Pull	Band	25reps	4sets
Overhead Pull	8lbs	15reps	4sets
Day #3: Biceps, Triceps and Shoulders:			
Close Grip Curl	8lbs	15reps	4sets
Hammer Curls	8lbs	15reps	4sets
Overhead Ext.	8lbs	15reps	4sets
Dips		until failure!!!!!!!!	
Incline Lat Raise	8-10lbs	15-20reps	3sets
Upright Row	8lbs	15reps	3sets
ENJOY!!!!!!!			

Figure 10.7 The scanned image opens as a PDF in Acrobat.

Capturing and Editing Images and Text

The PDF that you just created is simply an image file. Even if it contains text, all you have is a picture of text; the file is not recognized by the computer as text and the text can't be edited, searched, or indexed. To remedy this situation, you need to capture the document with Acrobat's Paper Capture. This process turns scanned text into editable text and images into stand-alone image objects within the document. The technical term for this is *optical character recognition,* or *OCR.*

Capture looks at any scanned-in artwork and text on a page and converts the text to editable text within Acrobat, preserving the document's layout. The benefit of this conversion is that now the text (as characters) takes up drastically less space than a comparable scan of the same text.

To prepare a document for Paper Capture, you must scan according to these parameters:

◆ 200–600 dpi for black-and-white images (300 usually is best)

◆ 200–400 dpi for color or grayscale images

If you don't follow those specifications, Paper Capture will give you error messages.

✔ Tip

■ If you have large numbers of documents to convert to PDFs, you might consider investing in Adobe's Acrobat Capture program. The industrial-strength version operates as a server application, which several users can access over a network.

Setting Capture Options

As Paper Capture converts text from images into editable text, it needs to know what sort of language and alphabet it should be looking for. You can choose the language in the Paper Capture Settings dialog box. You can also decide how fine you want the resolution of downsampled images and choose what style the output should be.

To change Paper Capture settings:

1. Choose Document > Paper Capture > Start Capture.

   The Paper Capture dialog box appears.

2. Click the Edit button (**Figure 10.8**).

   The Paper Capture Settings dialog box opens, with the default PDF Output Style showing (**Figure 10.9**).

3. From the pop-up menus, make choices to specify the language that Capture should look for, the output style, and the resolution of downsampled images.

4. Click OK.

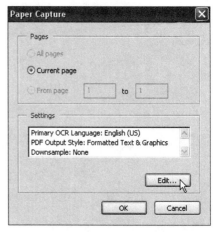

Figure 10.8 Click the Edit button to change the Paper Capture settings.

Figure 10.9 In the Paper Capture Settings dialog box, change any of the settings and click OK.

SETTING CAPTURE OPTIONS

Figure 10.10 Use the TouchUp Text tool to edit the captured text.

Figure 10.11 You can find one at a time or All Suspects in the captured text.

Working with Scanned Text

If you want to be able to edit the text you've scanned into Acrobat, you can convert an Adobe PDF image-only file to one of three formats:

◆ **Formatted Text and Graphics,** used for most standard PDF files, replaces bitmapped text with editable text in actual fonts that look similar to the ones in the original document.

◆ **Searchable Image (Exact)** retains the bitmapped appearance of the original document, and the searchable text is supplied on an invisible layer below the bitmap.

◆ **Searchable Image (Compact)** segments the original image to allow different areas to be compressed, sacrificing image quality but resulting in a smaller file.

To choose a capture format:

1. Choose Document > Paper Capture > Start Capture to open the Paper Capture dialog box.

2. In the Paper Capture dialog box, click the Edit button (**Figure 10.10**) to access the other formats.

   You'll find all three choices in the PDF Output Style pop-up menu (**Figure 10.11**).

3. Once you make your choice, click OK to return to the Paper Capture dialog box, and from there click OK to start the paper capture.

To convert scanned text to editable text:

1. Open the scanned image file, which you saved in PDF format.

2. Choose Document > Paper Capture > Start Capture.

   The Paper Capture dialog box appears (**Figure 10.12**).

3. Select Current Page.

   If you want to capture more than one page, either select All Pages to capture each page or select Specified Range to capture specific pages (for example, pages 4–8).

4. Click OK.

   When the conversion is finished, the document appears in captured form.

Figure 10.13 shows a PDF document before being captured, and **Figure 10.14** shows the same document after being captured. The most noticeable difference between a PDF before and after being captured is that the background of the scanned document is slightly gray instead of pure white like the background of the converted file. And, of course, you can select and edit text in the captured document.

Figure 10.12 The Paper Capture dialog box appears.

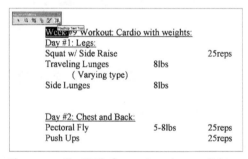

Figure 10.13 The PDF before capture shows a slight gray background and pixilated text.

Week #9 Workout: **Cardio** with weights:
Day #1: **Lees:**
Squat w/ Side Raise
Traveling Lunges   8lbs
          (Varying type)
Side Lunges   8lbs

Figure 10.14 After Capture, the text looks like normal text and the background is white.

Figure 10.15 Use the TouchUp Text tool to edit the captured text.

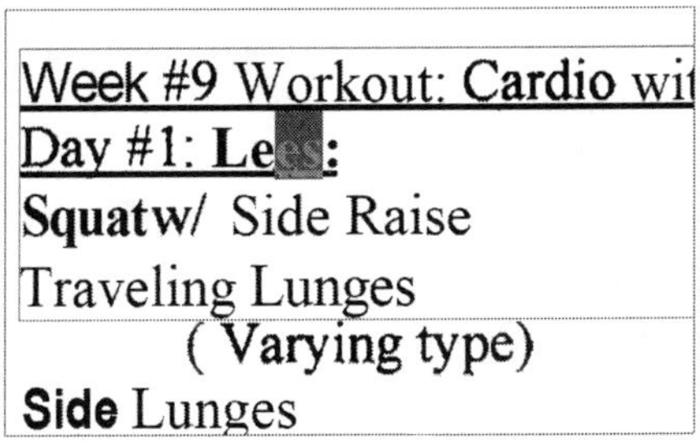

Week #9 Workout: Cardio wit

Day #1: Lees:

Squatw/ Side Raise

Traveling Lunges
            (Varying type)

Side Lunges

Figure 10.16 Select the text to be edited.

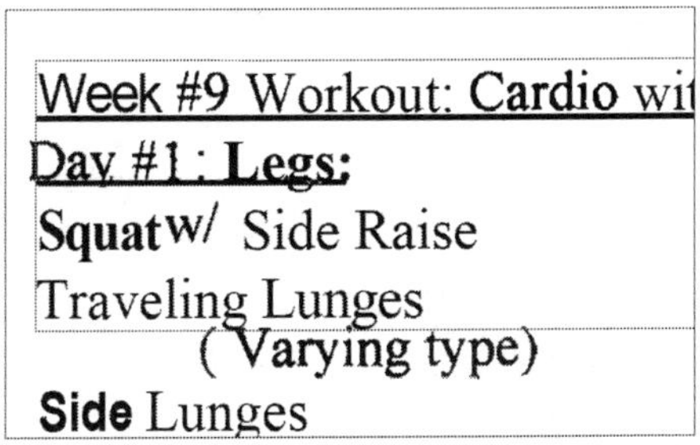

Week #9 Workout: Cardio wit

Day #1 : **Legs:**

Squatw/ Side Raise

Traveling Lunges
            (Varying type)

Side Lunges

Figure 10.17 The offending character is quickly changed.

To edit captured text:

1. Choose the TouchUp Text tool from the Advanced Editing toolbar (**Figure 10.15**). If it isn't visible, choose View > Toolbars > Advanced Editing.

2. Select the text you'd like to edit (**Figure 10.16**).

   Because the text is now editable, you can change letters, spelling, and punctuation by selecting the characters to be changed and typing over them.

3. Type the replacement character(s) (**Figure 10.17**).

4. To continue reading the document, switch back to the Hand tool by choosing it from the toolbar.

WORKING WITH SCANNED TEXT

Working with Suspects

Occasionally, Acrobat's Capture plug-in has trouble interpreting a word or character. In such cases, Acrobat substitutes what it thinks is correct and marks the word or character as a *suspect*. This section shows you how to review the suspects within a captured PDF.

To find and review suspects:

1. Choose Document > Paper Capture > Find All OCR Suspects (**Figure 10.18**).

   The suspect words appear in the Acrobat window, outlined with red rectangles (**Figure 10.19**).

2. Choose Document > Paper Capture > Find First OCR Suspect.

   The Find Element dialog box opens (**Figure 10.20**), displaying the suspect element.

3. To accept Acrobat's interpretation, click the Accept and Find button.

   If you don't accept the suspect, you can leave the bitmapped image in place, but you can't edit it later. It's best to accept the interpretation, so it will become editable text, then use the TouchUp Text tool to edit the text. See Chapter 8 for more information on editing text with the TouchUp Text tool.

4. Continue through the document until all suspects are dealt with.

Figure 10.18 You can find one suspect at a time or all suspects in the captured text.

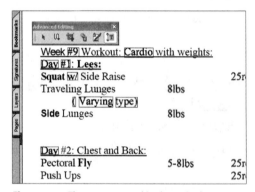

Figure 10.19 The suspect word is shown in the Acrobat window with red around it.

Figure 10.20 The Find Element dialog box appears.

DIGITAL SIGNATURES

The digital signature is becoming the standard for signing important electronic documents and perhaps soon will carry the authority of a handwritten signature. Acrobat 6.0 offers users the ability to create a digital signature, which can be one of three things: a handwritten name, a logo or symbol graphic, or text. Not only can you create a digital signature and sign PDF documents digitally, but you can verify that signature's authenticity. Also, if you sign a PDF digitally, you can veto changes made in the document after you signed it. Acrobat Self-Sign Security is Acrobat's default signature handler, but you can choose to install a different program.

Handling Digital Signatures

Acrobat's Self-Sign Security program is the default signature handler for Acrobat 6. It reads the assigned profile for each signature to verify and secure it, and includes both a private and a public key for creating and verifying signatures. The private key is password-protected so that only the user can sign the document. The public key is used to verify the authenticity of the signature and is embedded in the PDF document. New to Acrobat 6 is support for Microsoft's code signing and digital security with MS CAPI.

The first step in creating a digital signature is to choose a signature handler.

To set a default signature handler:

1. Choose Edit/Acrobat > Preferences (Ctrl+K/Command+K) to open the General pane of the Preferences window.

2. Select Digital Signatures in the list on the left (**Figure 11.1**).

3. Choose a signature handler from the "Default Method to use when signing" pop-up menu.

   Unless you install an alternative program, the only choice will be Default Certificate Security.

4. Check the "Verify signatures when document is opened" check box to make sure the signatures are authentic when you open a document (**Figure 11.2**).

5. Click OK to accept the changes and close Preferences.

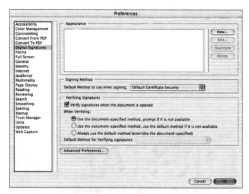

Figure 11.1 Select Digital Signatures in the list on the left side of the General Preferences window.

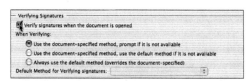

Figure 11.2 Click the Verify Signatures When Document Is Opened check box.

✔ Tip

- You can install third-party digital-signature creation and verification handlers by using an installer or copying the signature handler plug-in into the Acrobat Plug-Ins directory. A good example of an installer-based handler is VeriSign, available free from PlanetPDF (www.pdfstore.com).

Figure 11.3 Choose Advanced > Manage Digital ID > My Digital ID Files > Select My Digital ID File.

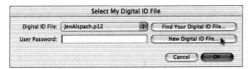

Figure 11.4 Click the New Digital ID File button to start a new digital ID.

Figure 11.5 Read the disclaimer before clicking Continue.

Setting up a Signature Profile

The next step in creating a digital signature is to set up a signature profile. The profile you set up will be password-protected; it is your own private key. When you save the profile, the key will be embedded in the documents you sign. If you sign documents in two roles—those of president and treasurer, for example—you'll need to set up two separate profiles. Because the information contained in your profiles is so crucial, it's a good idea to make backup copies of the profiles as soon as you create them.

To create a profile:

1. Choose Advanced > Manage Digital ID > My Digital ID Files > Select My Digital ID File (**Figure 11.3**).

   This opens the Select My Digital ID File dialog box.

2. Click the New Digital ID File button (**Figure 11.4**).

   A disclaimer pops up, asking you if you want to continue (**Figure 11.5**).

3. Click Continue to bring up the Create Self-Signed Digital ID dialog box.

(continues on next page)

SETTING UP A SIGNATURE PROFILE

4. Enter your information in the Digital ID Details and the Digital ID File Security sections; click Create (**Figure 11.6**).

5. Enter a name and save location for your new profile in the New Self-Sign Digital ID File dialog box (**Figure 11.7**), and click Save.

✔ Tips

- By default, you'll save your profile to My Documents/Adobe/Acrobat (Windows) or Documents:Profiles (Mac). Acrobat creates these directories automatically.

- On Windows computers, you don't need to set a password as you do on a Macintosh, as shown in Figure 11.6. Acrobat uses Windows Certificate Security Method, used with your Windows login.

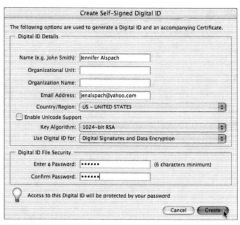

Figure 11.6 Enter your information in the Digital ID Details and Digital ID File Security sections.

Figure 11.7 Click Save to store your signature profile.

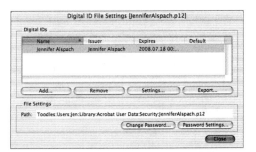

Figure 11.8 This dialog box informs you that you're logged in.

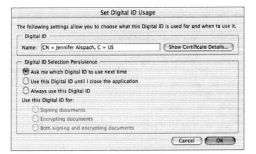

Figure 11.9 Open the Set Digital ID Usage dialog box to change any aspects of your profile.

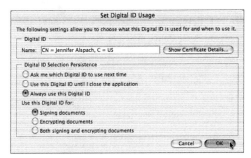

Figure 11.10 The new settings call for this digital ID to be the default.

To edit a profile:

1. Log in with your user name by choosing Advanced > Manage Digital ID > My Digital ID File Settings.

   The Select My Digital ID File dialog box appears.

2. Enter your password, and click OK.

   The Digital ID File Settings dialog box appears, showing your Digital ID (**Figure 11.8**).

3. Select your Digital ID name, then click the Settings button.

   The Set Digital ID Usage dialog box appears (**Figure 11.9**).

4. Change any of the settings for how and when your digital signature is used (**Figure 11.10**).

5. Click OK.

Creating a Digital Signature

After you've created and saved your profile, you can create the actual signature that you'll affix to documents.

To add a handwritten signature or logo to a profile:

1. Scan your signature or logo into a bitmap graphics program (such as Adobe Photoshop) or use a program like Adobe Illustrator to create your signature or logo and then save it as a PDF.

2. Choose Edit/Acrobat > Preferences (Ctrl+K/Command+K) to open the General pane of the Preferences window.

3. Select Digital Signatures in the list on the left, and click the New button in the Appearance area of the Digital Signatures Preferences (**Figure 11.11**).

   This brings up the Configure Signature Appearance dialog box (**Figure 11.12**).

4. Type a title for the signature, and click the PDF File button in the Configure Graphic section.

   The Select Picture dialog box appears.

5. Click the Browse button (**Figure 11.13**) to find your PDF file.

   The Open dialog box appears.

6. Navigate to the PDF file of your signature that you saved, and click the Select button.

   You return to the Select Picture dialog box.

7. Click OK.

   You see a preview of the graphic (**Figure 11.14**).

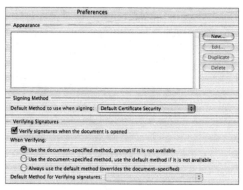

Figure 11.11 Open the preferences for digital signatures.

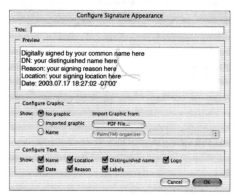

Figure 11.12 The New button brings up the Configure Signature Appearance dialog box.

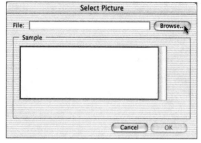

Figure 11.13 Click the Browse button to find your graphic.

Figure 11.14 When you have your graphic selected, click OK to see a preview of the graphic.

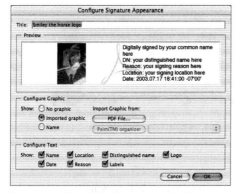

Figure 11.15 You can configure the text in the Configure Signature Appearance dialog box.

8. Click OK to close the Select Picture dialog box and return to the Configure Signature Appearance dialog box.

9. Click OK to return to the Digital Signature area in Preferences.

10. Click OK to accept your changes and close Preferences.

✔ Tip

- In the Configure Text section of the Configure Signature Appearance dialog box (**Figure 11.15**) you can choose to have additional information displayed along with your signature. This information includes the date, reason for signing, the location, and distinguished name (such as Doctor, Captain, or Madam).

To remove a signature from a profile:

1. Log in with your user name by choosing Advanced > Manage Digital ID > My Digital ID File Settings.

2. Choose Edit/Acrobat > Preferences (Ctrl+K/Command+K) to open the General pane of the Preferences window.

3. Select Digital Signatures in the list on the left.

4. Choose an Appearance in the Appearance list box, and click Delete.

No alert appears, the signature is automatically deleted, so be sure you really want to do this.

5. Click OK to accept your changes and close Preferences.

✔ Tip

- You can also edit or duplicate the signature in the Appearance section of the Digital Signature Preferences dialog box.

CREATING A DIGITAL SIGNATURE

Signing Documents

Now that you can create signatures, it's time to sign your document. Once you have your signature, digital ID, and profiles set, you can sign your PDF files with confidence.

To sign a document:

1. Read through a document that needs your signature to ensure that you know what you are signing.

2. Click the Signatures tab on the left side of the document window (**Figure 11.16**).

3. Choose Create a Blank Signature Field from the Options menu (**Figure 11.17**).

   A message comes up saying that a signature field was created and telling you to click and drag with the mouse to set the area for the signature field (**Figure 11.18**). After you do this, the Digital Signature Properties dialog box appears.

Figure 11.16 Click the Signatures tab to access Signatures.

Figure 11.17 Create a blank signature field first before adding your signature.

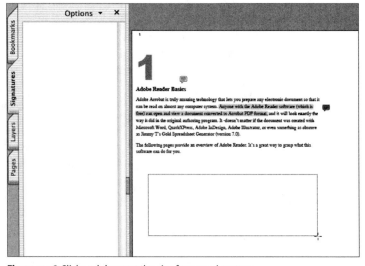

Figure 11.18 Click and drag out the size for your signature.

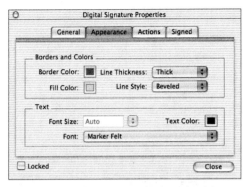

Figure 11.19 Enter your options for the style of the signature box.

Figure 11.20 Choose Sign Signature Field from the Options menu in the Signatures pane.

Figure 11.21 Click the Continue Signing button.

4. Select the options you want in the Appearance tab, such as line weight, color, and style and fill color for the box. You can also select font and other text options (**Figure 11.19**).

5. Click Close to close the Signature Properties dialog box.

6. In the Signatures panel on the left side of your document window, select a signature name.

7. Choose Sign Signature Field from the Options menu (**Figure 11.20**).

   An alert box opens, saying you're about to apply the first digital signature to this document.

8. Click Continue Signing (**Figure 11.21**). This opens the Apply Signature to Document dialog box.

(continues on next page)

9. In the Apply Signature to Document dialog box, confirm your password and click Sign and Save (**Figure 11.22**).

A note comes up saying you have successfully signed the document, and your signature appears in the Signatures pane and on the document (**Figure 11.23**).

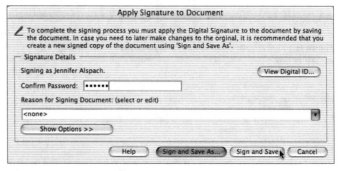

Figure 11.22 Click the Sign and Save button.

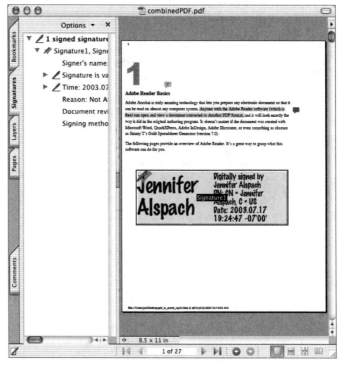

Figure 11.23 Now your signature is in the document.

PDF Files and the Web

The World Wide Web has transformed the entire world into an HTML-based society of Internet junkies. It wouldn't be too bad if HTML were compact, flexible, and produced good-looking content, but that's not always the case. Professional Web designers and amateurs alike know that browser differences can distort the most carefully designed page. Add the unpredictability of Web viewers' monitor settings, and you have a desperate need for a stable, dependable format for documents: hence, PDF.

PDFs are everywhere on the Internet: as eBooks, order forms on retail sites, help files, and even downloadable tax forms. When the IRS adopts your technology, you know you've really arrived.

This chapter discusses how to use Acrobat and PDF files on the Web, from reading pages online to creating and displaying them on your own Web server.

Reading PDF Pages Online

PDF files can be viewed live on the Internet by Netscape and Internet Explorer Web browsers. If the Web server hosting the pages is configured properly, and the PDFs themselves are optimized, the pages are sent one at a time, so a reader who wants to view only pages 1, 3, 16, and 243 doesn't have to download the entire 300-page document. Normally, the Acrobat or Reader Installer configures your Web browsers to read PDFs online, but this section shows you how to set up your browser manually, just in case. These are the options you set in Acrobat Preferences:

* **Display PDF in Browser** will let you view PDFs in your Web browser. If it isn't checked, Acrobat will launch and display the PDF.

* **Check Browser Settings when Starting Acrobat** checks for application compatibility every time you launch the application.

* **Allow Fast Web View** will display one page at a time rather than waiting until the whole document is downloaded.

* **Allow Speculative Downloading in the Background** will stop the background downloading visibility when you do any task in Acrobat.

* **Connection Speed** allows you to choose your Internet connection speed.

* **Internet Settings** allows you to set up your Internet connection.

Figure 12.1 Check your options.

Figure 12.2. To view the Adobe PDF toolbar, choose View > Toolbars > Adobe PDF.

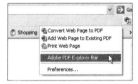

Figure 12.3 Choose Adobe PDF Explorer Bar.

Figure 12.4 The PDF Explorer displays your computer and its contents for easy browsing.

To set up your Web browser to read PDF files (Windows):

1. Choose Edit > Preferences.

   Choose Internet from the list on the left.

2. Make sure Display PDF in Browser is checked. If you don't have this option checked, the PDF will open in Acrobat (**Figure 12.1**).

3. Change any other options as necessary, and click OK.

To view a test PDF document in your browser:

1. Launch your Web browser.

2. Choose View > Toolbars > Adobe PDF (**Figure 12.2**).

3. Choose Adobe PDF Explorer Bar from the Adobe PDF menu (**Figure 12.3**). This lets you navigate your computer in the left pane and choose a PDF file to open or convert (**Figure 12.4**).

4. Find the PDF you want to open in your browser and double-click it.

   The PDF page appears in your Web browser.

✔ Tips

■ Acrobat will load as an application in the background, so you'll need enough free RAM to run your browser and the Acrobat application at the same time.

■ Most PDF files have the extension .pdf. In fact, if they don't, your Web browser won't recognize them as PDFs.

Editing PDFs Online

You can also edit PDFs within a Web browser, just as you would with Acrobat. This is especially useful when you're collaborating on work, because several different people can add comments to the same document, and see each others' comments as well.

Be aware, however, that you can't edit just any old PDF that your browser displays. The PDF must be hosted on a server that's properly configured, which is beyond the scope of this book. Consult your network administrator if you need to set up PDFs for online editing, and refer to Chapter 9 for more on commenting and reviewing.

To add comments to a document:

1. Open a PDF document in your Web browser.

2. Select the Note tool in the Commenting toolbar.

3. In the document, drag a marquee around the area where you want to add a note (**Figure 12.5**).

    A note box appears.

4. Enter the text of the note.

5. Expand the Comments List, if necessary, by clicking the Comments tab on the left.

    You see the page reference to the note you added (**Figure 12.6**).

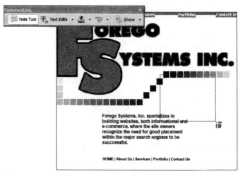

Figure 12.5 Drag a marquee around the area in which you want to create a note.

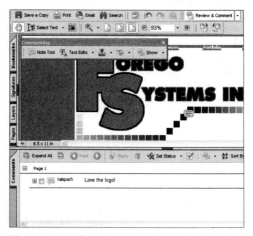

Figure 12.6 You'll see the page reference to the note you added.

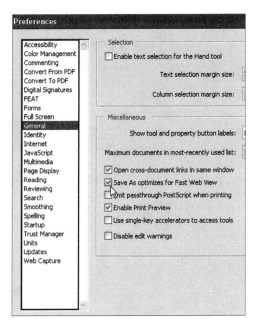

Figure 12.7 Check the Save As optimizes for Fast Web View check box, if it isn't already checked.

Optimizing PDF Files for Online Viewing

When a Web server delivers a PDF one page at a time, it's called *byte-serving*. In order for byte-serving to work, the PDF files must first be optimized. In previous versions of Acrobat, you had to select optimization as an option at the time you saved the file. Acrobat 6.0 lets you set optimization as the default behavior.

To optimize PDF files for byte-serving:

1. Choose Edit > Preferences (Ctrl-K/ Command-K), to open Acrobat Preferences.

2. In the list on the left side of the window, select General.

3. Make sure that the Save As optimizes for Fast Web View check box is checked (**Figure 12.7**).

4. Click OK.

   Any file you save will now automatically be optimized, and the document will be displayed one page at a time.

   (continues on next page)

OPTIMIZING PDF FILES FOR ONLINE VIEWING

✔ **Tips**

- Your Web administrator can probably tell you whether your Web site is set up to byte-serve PDF files. If not, explain that you'd like to byte-serve PDF files, and the administrator will probably be able to upgrade the server software or direct you to a Web server that can byte-serve.

- In some cases, you may prefer viewers to download an entire document, instead of a page at a time. For example, with the entire document on their systems, viewers will be able to access individual pages much faster than if the pages have to be downloaded individually. To provide this capability, you must create non-optimized files, which you do by simply unchecking the Save As optimizes for Fast Web View check box in the General area of Preferences.

OPTIMIZING PDF FILES FOR ONLINE VIEWING

ACROBAT HELP

Figure A.1 The Windows Help menu.

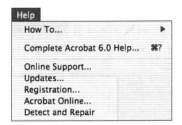

Figure A.2 The Macintosh Help menu.

As much as we like to think we know about a program, we always need help. In the Help menu, Adobe Acrobat offers several choices for a little assistance. The choices differ for Windows and Macintosh (**Figures A.1** and **A.2**).

This menu is the main feature you'll use to get help with Acrobat. To access Help, choose Complete Acrobat 6.0 Help from the Help menu (F1/Command+?).

Using Contents

When Adobe Acrobat Help opens, it displays tabs for the three main sections of the file in the pane on the left: Contents, Search, and Index (**Figure A.3**). Each tab has access to the same topics; which one you use depends on your preferred work style. Each topic in the Help file is bookmarked so that you can jump to it quickly. To help you find specific items, bookmarks are grouped hierarchically in the Help pane.

To use Contents:

1. Click the Contents tab at the top of the Help pane (**Figure A.4**).

   You go to a page that lists the main topics in the Help file, with links to each topic.

2. Click the triangle to the left of a bookmark to display the list of chapters in the Contents pane (**Figure A.5**).

   Each chapter has its own triangle, indicating further levels exist deeper in the hierarchy.

Using Contents

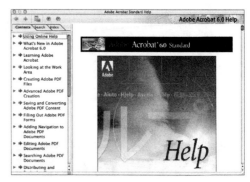

Figure A.3 The Acrobat Help document includes tabs for the main sections.

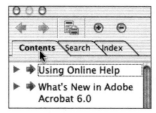

Figure A.4 Click the Contents tab in the Help pane.

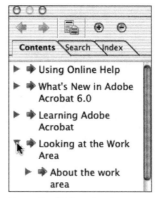

Figure A.5 Click a triangle to display a list of subtopics.

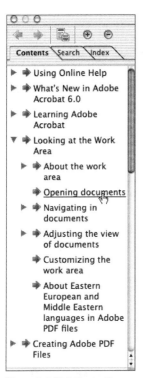

Figure A.6 Click the topic you want to view.

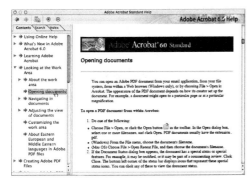

Figure A.7 Acrobat displays the page for that topic.

Figure A.8 You can increase or decrease the magnification.

3. Click the topic in the Contents pane that you want to view (**Figure A.6**).

Acrobat displays the page for that topic in the Document pane (**Figure A.7**).

Acrobat provides a back button (which takes you to the last page you viewed) and the option to print the topic as well as to zoom in or out of the topic pane (**Figure A.8**).

Using the Index

The Index is my favorite way to find information on a subject in Acrobat. It's quicker than scrolling through a table of contents or using the Search tab.

To search with the Index:

1. Click the Index tab.

   Letters appear in the Index pane, with arrows indicating nested topics (**Figure A.9**).

2. Click the letter that corresponds to the first letter in the topic on which you want to get information.

   All the topics under that letter appear in the pane.

3. When you find the topic, click it (**Figure A.10**) to go to that page in the Help document.

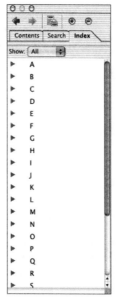

Figure A.9 Click the letter that corresponds to the first letter of the topic on which you want information.

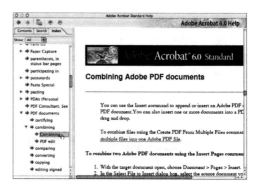

Figure A.10 Click the desired title to display that topic's information.

USING THE INDEX

Figure A.11 Click the Search button to find your entered topic.

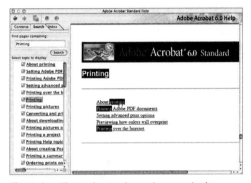

Figure A.12 The topic you chose shows up in the Help pane.

Using Search

You can type a word or words in the Search tab of Help to find help on a specific topic. Search is handy if you already know the exact wording of the Help topics or the general thread, such as PDF or Printing, but for more obscure topics, you're better off using the Index.

To use Search:

1. In the Help pane, click the Search tab.

2. In the text box, enter the topic you wish to find Help on. I typed Printing for this example.

3. Click the Search button (**Figure A.11**). The search results are listed in the left pane.

4. Click the topic you wish to view and it shows up in the Document pane, with the search term highlighted (**Figure A.12**).

USING SEARCH

Printing Help Topics

You can print any of the topics you're reading, for future reference.

To print Help topics:

1. Select the topic you want to print.

2. Click the Print Topic button at the top of the left-hand window.

   The Print dialog box appears (**Figure A.13**), with the appropriate page numbers already filled in.

3. Click the Print button to print the topic.

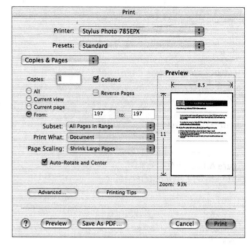

Figure A.13 Printing a Help topic is as easy as printing any other PDF document.

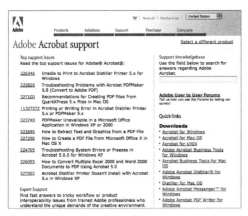

Figure A.14 Choosing Online Support takes you to Adobe's online support Web page.

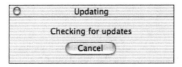

Figure A.15 Updates will automatically check online for any updates to the software.

Other Help Menu Items

Although one could argue that these aren't Help in the strictest sense, it's undeniable that one-click connections to information, updates, and online registration are wonderful features.

- ◆ **Online Support** takes you to the Online Support Web page (**Figure A.14**), where you can check for updates and new add-ons for Acrobat and link to the top support issues.

- ◆ **Updates** has Acrobat look online for any updates to the Acrobat 6.0 Standard application (**Figure A.15**).

- ◆ **Online Registration** lets you register your copy of Acrobat instantly. Acrobat starts your Web browser and takes you to the registration page on Adobe's Web site (**Figure A.16**).

- ◆ **Acrobat Online** takes you directly to Adobe's Acrobat home page (**Figure A.17**). From there, choose any of the topics you want to know more about.

(continues on next page)

Figure A.16 You can register your copy of Acrobat online.

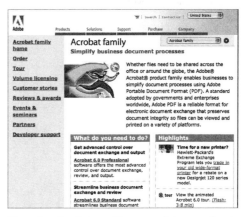

Figure A.17 Acrobat provides a one-click connection to the Acrobat home page.

OTHER HELP MENU ITEMS

207

◆ **Detect and Repair** looks for any missing components of the Acrobat 6 Standard application. If it finds missing components, it will repair them and open an alert box (**Figure A.18**).

These additional items are offered in the Windows Help menu. On Macintosh, these items are found under the Acrobat menu.

◆ **About Acrobat 6.0** displays the Acrobat splash screen, which lists the team that created Acrobat, the release version, the person to whom the copy is licensed, and the serial number. Click the splash screen to remove it.

◆ **About Adobe Plug-Ins** opens the About Adobe Plug-Ins dialog box (**Figure A.19**), which lists all the standard Acrobat plug-ins. Select a plug-in from the list on the left, and Acrobat displays information on it on the right side of the dialog box. Click OK to exit.

◆ **About Third-Party Plug-Ins** lets you choose PrintMe Internet Printing from the submenu. The PrintMe Networks dialog box appears (**Figure A.20**), explaining the ease of using PrintMe and about the PrintMe plug-in.

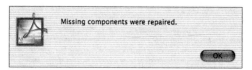

Figure A.18 Detect and Repair keeps Acrobat running smoothly.

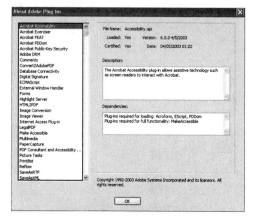

Figure A.19 Choosing About Adobe Acrobat Plug-Ins from the Help menu brings up the About Adobe Plug-Ins dialog box.

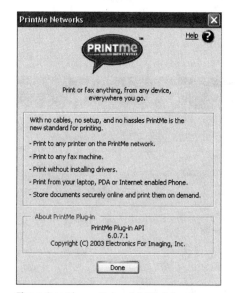

Figure A.20 Choose Help > PrintMe Internet Printing to see how easy it is to use the PrintMe plug-in.

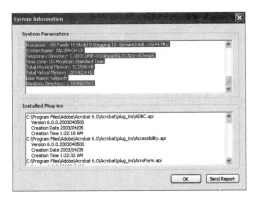

Figure A.21 This box displays the Windows system information.

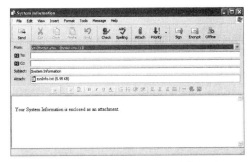

Figure A.22 You can email your system information to someone else.

◆ **System Info** displays information about your computer (**Figure A.21**). (On Macs, click About This Mac under the Apple menu to get this type of information.) You can send a report about the system information, for example, to your IT person, by clicking Send Report. This launches your email program with your system information attached (**Figure A.22**).

✔ Tip

■ You can find a list of Adobe-approved third-party plug-ins at Adobe's Web site (www.adobe.com/products/plugins/acrobat/main.html).

Using the How To Area

The How To area is new to Acrobat 6.0. Choose a topic, and this wonderful new feature walks you through how to do it. If the How To pane on the right is not visible, choose Help > How To > How To Window. These basic topics are listed in the pane: Create PDF, Review & Comment, Secure, Sign, More Topics, and Complete Acrobat 6.0 Help (**Figure A.23**).

◆ **Create PDF** brings up a list of subtopics, from which you can choose what you want to do (**Figure A.24**). The topics cover all the various ways to create PDFs, including from a file, from a Web site, from a scanned document, and from MS Office or other applications.

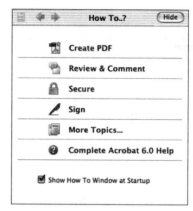

Figure A.23 The How To pane takes you through a variety of tasks.

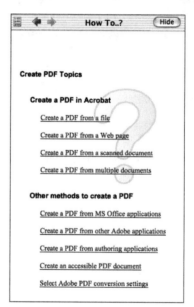

Figure A.24 One of the main topics is Create PDF.

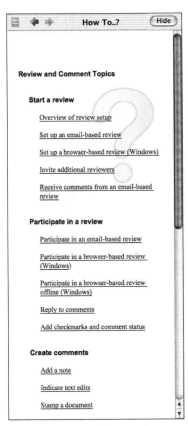

Figure A.25 These topics cover the whole process of reviewing PDFs.

- **Review & Comment** takes you through the reviewing and commenting process (**Figure A.25**), from setting up a review to editing text and dealing with comments.

- **Secure** covers how to create a certified document, add a document password, and restrict printing or changes to a document (**Figure A.26**).

- **Sign** goes through how to set up a digital ID, create a blank signature field, sign a document, change a signature appearance, share certificate information, get another user's certificate information, and validate signatures (**Figure A.27**).

(continues on next page)

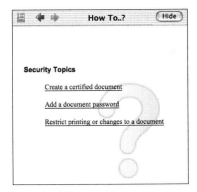

Figure A.26 Figure out how to secure your PDF.

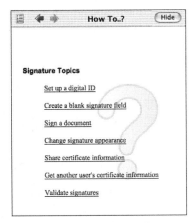

Figure A.27 Go here to find out how to sign your PDF documents.

USING THE HOW TO AREA

◆ **More Topics** covers miscellaneous topics that fall under areas like editing documents, navigating and structuring PDFs, eBooks, dealing with forms, and improving documents' accessibility (**Figure A.28**).

◆ **Complete Acrobat Help** launches the Acrobat Help document as shown in **Figure A.29**. As mentioned earlier, you can also access Acrobat Help by choosing Help > Complete Acrobat 6.0 Help or pressing F1/Command+?.

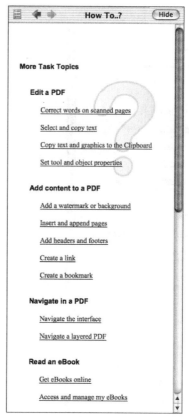

Figure A.28 More Topics lists miscellaneous tasks.

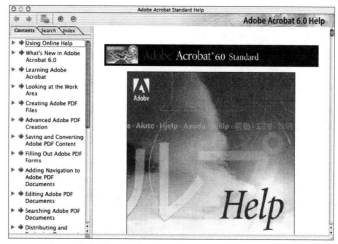

Figure A.29 Complete Acrobat Help can also be accessed through the How To pane.

USING THE HOW TO AREA

DOCUMENT SECURITY

Are you concerned that your document may fall into the wrong hands or that readers may try to change your prose? Or maybe you'd like to distribute your document electronically but don't want that document to be printed and possibly distributed to unauthorized users.

Acrobat's built-in security options can prevent unauthorized access, printing, and editing of your PDF files. Secured PDF files stand up to rigorous attempts to bypass their password-protection schemes.

Setting Security Options

By default, PDF documents are open, meaning that anyone can open the file, make changes, resave it, copy text and images from it, and work with the file as his or her own. You must add security options to a PDF document manually. A PDF file can have two types of password security: one for opening the file, and one for altering or copying it. The Security submenu of the Document menu contains the following options:

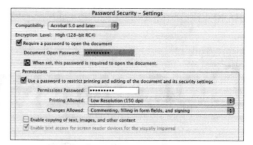

Figure B.1 This dialog box is where you set most of the security options for your document.

*   **Restrict Opening and Editing** opens the Password Security Settings dialog box (**Figure B.1**), where you can set the compatibility according to the version of Acrobat. You can also set the encryption level, password requirements, and permissions for printing, changes, access for screen reader devices for the visually impaired, enable plaintext metadata, and copying of text, images, and content.

*   **Encrypt for Certain Identities using Certificates** lets you set a digital ID to access the encrypted PDF. For more on setting digital IDs and signatures, see Chapter 11.

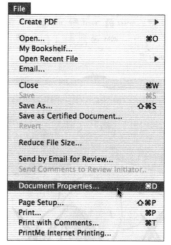

Figure B.2 Choose Document Properties from the File menu.

*   **Display Restrictions and Security** opens up the Document Properties dialog box with the Security option selected. The dialog box displays the restrictions and security set for this particular PDF.

To set password security options:

1. Open the document you want to protect.

2. Choose File > Document Properties (Ctrl+D/Command+D) (**Figure B.2**). The Document Properties dialog box appears.

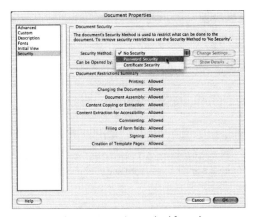

Figure B.3 Choose a security method from the pop-up menu.

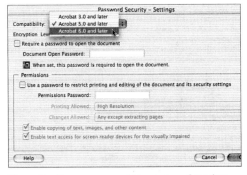

Figure B.4 Choose a compatible version of Acrobat.

Figure B.5 Check Permissions Password if you want to restrict the printing and editing of your PDF.

3. Choose Security from the list on the left side.

The Document Security options are displayed on the right side of the Document Properties dialog box.

4. Choose a security method (No Security, Password Security, or Certificate Security) from the pop-up menu (**Figure B.3**). I chose Password Security, which launches the Password Security Settings dialog box.

5. Choose an Acrobat version for compatibility (**Figure B.4**).

6. Check the "Require a password to open the document" box.

7. Enter a password.

8. If you'd like to enter a permissions password, check the "Use a password to restrict printing and editing of the document and security settings" box (**Figure B.5**).

(continues on next page)

SETTING SECURITY OPTIONS

9. Enter a password and choose whether to allow printing and changes (**Figure B.6**).

10. Check the other boxes according to whether you want to enable copying of text, images, and other content, enable text access for screen reader devices for the visually impaired, and enable plain-text metadata.

11. Click OK. This brings up the Adobe Acrobat—Confirm Open Document Password dialog box. Reenter the password you set in step 9 and click OK (**Figure B.7**).

    A warning box comes up (**Figure B.8**) alerting you that security settings will not be applied until the document has been saved and closed. Click OK.

12. Save and close the file.

    At this point, the document is locked. The only way to reopen it is to supply the password (**Figure B.9**).

✔ Tip

■ Acrobat has no limit on the length of a password, but the password is case-sensitive.

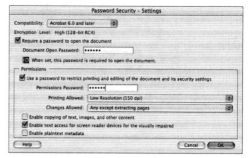

Figure B.6 Enter a password and your printing and editing choices.

Figure B.7 Once you click OK, you have to reenter your password.

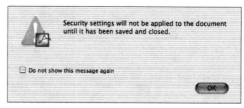

Figure B.8 A box comes up warning you that you need to save and close the file for your security changes to take effect.

Figure B.9 When you open a secured document, you'll need to enter the password first.

Figure B.10 A warning comes up, making sure you want to remove security.

To remove security from a document:

1. Open the document, using the password.

2. Choose File > Document Properties. The Document Properties dialog box appears.

3. Choose Security from the list on the left.

4. Choose No Security from the Security Method pop-up menu. A warning box comes asking if you're sure you want to remove security for this document (**Figure B.10**). Click OK.

5. Click the Close button. Now the document can be opened without a password.

How to Choose a Password

If keeping your document secure is important, the most important thing you can do is have a good password. When you choose a password, keep the following rules in mind:

- Don't write it down anywhere. If you can't remember a password, don't use it.

- Don't pick an easy guesser, such as the name of a child, friend, pet, or spouse.

- Combine numerals and letters. If you use only numbers in an eight-character password, 10 million combinations are possible. If you use a combination of eight letters and numbers, the combinations total almost 3 trillion.

SETTING SECURITY OPTIONS

Other standard security options

Besides allowing you to prevent a document from being opened without a password, Acrobat provides several other types of protection.

When setting the permissions for printing and changes, you have a few other choices. Under the Printing Allowed pop-up menu, choose from high resolution or low resolution (150 dpi). Under the Changes allowed pop-up menu, choose from these options:

◆ **None** means that no one can make any changes to your PDF.

◆ **Inserting, deleting, and rotating pages** lets the user insert, delete, and rotate any pages in the PDF.

◆ **Filling in form fields and signing** is best when sending forms, so the user can fill in the form and sign the document.

◆ **Commenting, filling in form fields, and signing** lets the user comment on the file, fill in the form fields, and sign the PDF.

◆ **Any except extracting pages** lets the user do anything to the PDF except remove/extract pages.

Figure B.11 The Password dialog box appears asking for a password.

Figure B.12 If you enter the wrong password, you can click OK and try twice more.

Opening Secure PDFs

Opening a password-protected document, whether it's one that you protected or one you received from someone else, takes only a moment.

To open a locked PDF file:

1. Double-click the file's icon or select it in Acrobat's Open dialog box.

   The Password dialog box appears, notifying you that the document is protected by a password (**Figure B.11**).

2. Enter the password and click OK to open the document.

   If you enter the correct password, the document opens.

   If you enter the wrong password, an alert box appears (**Figure B.12**). Click OK to return to the Password dialog box; then enter the correct password and click OK.

✔ Tip

■ After a wrong password has been entered three times, the dialog box ceases to appear, and you must open the document again by double-clicking its icon or using Acrobat's Open dialog box.

OPENING SECURE PDFS

Checking Security Settings

After you open a locked document, you can find out which security settings the author of the document specified for the file. Then you'll know how much you're allowed to do with the file.

To check the security settings of a file:

1. Open the document for which you want to check security.

2. Choose File > Document Properties.
   The Document Properties dialog box appears.

3. Click Security in the list on the left to display all the options that are set for the open document (**Figure B.13**).

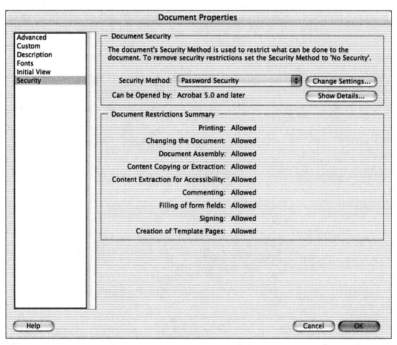

Figure B.13 In the Document Properties dialog box, click Security to see the security settings for the current document.

ACCESSIBILITY

Accessibility features enable users with motor and vision challenges to use PDF files with relative ease. The areas that accessibility covers are: speech (reading aloud), visibility, navigation, and keyboard.

Reading Out Loud

The Read Aloud feature converts text to spoken words. You can choose to have one page read, or the whole document, and you can choose the reading order. While a PDF is being read out loud, you can always pause or stop the reading. For more on this enhancement, see Chapter 2.

To set the Read Aloud options:

1. Choose File/Acrobat > Preferences.

2. Choose Reading from the list on the left. This displays the default reading preference settings (**Figure C.1**).

3. Set desired volume level.

4. Choose a voice.

   On Windows you only have the default voice. On the Macintosh, choose from a variety of voices. Keep in mind that some voices sound better than others. You can set the pitch and words per minute as well, on both Mac and Windows.

5. Choose a reading order from the pop-up menu (**Figure C.2**).

   ▲ **Infer Reading Order** is generally the best method for reading a document. This option reads in the order that the document was tagged. If the document isn't tagged, it will use the most logical reading order.

   ▲ **Left to Right/Top to Bottom Order** will read the PDF strictly from left to right and top to bottom, regardless of how the document was created.

   ▲ **Use Reading Order in Raw Print Stream** reads the words in the order they were recorded in the print stream.

6. Click OK.

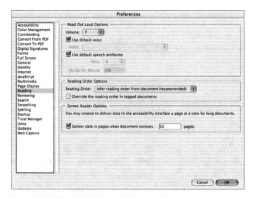

Figure C.1 The default Reading preferences.

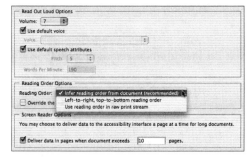

Figure C.2 Select a reading order.

READING OUT LOUD

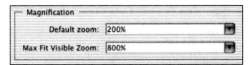

Figure C.3 Set the magnification of your document to something that will be helpful to visually challenged users.

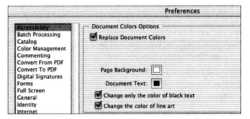

Figure C.4 The Accessibility area lets you set your document colors to be more visible than they might normally be.

Other Accessibility Options

There are a number of other simple things you can do to make your document more accessible to all readers. You'll find some of these features in Preferences, some in other areas of the program.

Visibility

One of the quickest ways to make your PDF more readable for people with vision challenges is to change its viewing options. When you first open a file, change the Default Zoom in the Page Display panel of Preferences (**Figure C.3**). For more on setting these preferences, see Chapter 2.

In the Accessibility panel of Preferences, you'll find other options that increase the visibility of text and graphics on your pages by changing the Document Colors Options (**Figure C.4**). For example, you can choose to replace the page background and text colors.

Automatic scrolling

Using the Automatic Scrolling feature lets you move through a PDF without relying on the mouse.

To scroll automatically:

1. With the document open, choose View > Automatically Scroll (**Figure C.5**).

   The document will start scrolling slowly down your screen.

2. Use the number keys to control the speed of the scrolling, with 9 being fast and 0 being slow.

3. Use the up and down arrow keys to change the direction of scrolling.

   You can also use the hyphen or minus key to go backward.

4. To go to the previous or next page, use the left or right arrows.

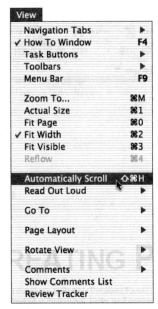

Figure C.5 You can choose to automatically scroll through documents, using the keyboard to control speed and direction of scrolling.

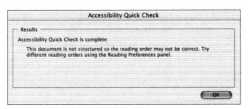

Figure C.6 This window shows the result of Acrobat's Accessibility Quick Check.

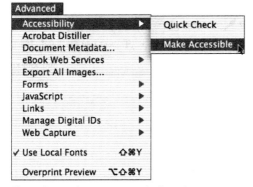

Figure C.7 Acrobat can automatically make your document more accessible.

Making Your PDF Accessible

You can check how accessible your PDF is. Acrobat will report on the following accessibility features: alternative text for figures, specified languages for text, reliable character encodings, and logical structural tree referencing for the contents of the PDF file.

To check for accessibility:

◆ Choose Advanced > Accessibility > Quick Check.

A window appears, with a brief report on the accessibility of your document (**Figure C.6**).

✔ Tip

■ If you need specific fixes for accessibility problems you'll need to upgrade to Acrobat 6.0 Professional for more options.

To make your PDF accessible:

1. Open the PDF you want to make accessible.

2. Choose Advanced > Accessibility > Make Accessible (**Figure C.7**).

   Figure C.8 shows the progress of making the file accessible.

   Your document won't look any different: The tagged areas are hidden in the background.

Figure C.8 When you make your file accessible you won't see any changes.

MAKING YOUR PDF ACCESSIBLE

INDEX

A

About Acrobat 6.0
   Macintosh Acrobat menu, 208
   Windows Help menu, 208
About Adobe Pug-Ins
   Macintosh Acrobat menu, 208
   Windows Help menu, 208
About Third-Party Plug-Ins
   Macintosh Acrobat menu, 208
   Windows Help menu, 208
Accessibility options, 221–225
Accessibility pane, 223
Accessibility preferences (Adobe Reader), 28
Accessible Text format, 85
Acrobat 6
   adding watermarks and backgrounds,
      82–83
   comment types, 134–136
   creating slide show, 119–121
   headers/footers
      adding, 80
      editing, 80
      removing/restoring, 81
   How To Area topics, 210–212
   menus, 70
   panes, 73–74
   opening Web links, 62
   showing/hiding layers, 78
   splitting window views, 77

starting/quitting, 68
toolbars, 69
Acrobat 6 Professional, 33, 225
Acrobat Capture, 179, 184
Acrobat Help
   Acrobat Online, 207
   Contents, 202–203
   Detect and Repair, 208
   Index, 204
   Online Registration, 207
   Online Support, 207
   printing Help topics, 206
   Search, 205
   Updates, 207
Acrobat icon, 2, 68
Acrobat Online, 207
Acrobat Plug in folder, 68
Acrobat splash screen, 68
actions
   attaching to bookmarks, 112
   links performing, 130
activating Palm OS device for eBooks, 53
Actual Size, zooming, 18
adding files, 57, 119
Add Note to Selected Text option, 140
Adding watermarks and backgrounds, 82–83
Adobe Acrobat. *See* Acrobat 6
Adobe Download Manager, 5
Adobe DRM Activator Web site, 40
Adobe eBooks Central, 41, 42

eBooks Online button, 42
editing links, 130
Edit menu
    Acrobat 6, 70
    Adobe Reader, 10
email
    document for review, 164
    eBooks, 54
    in Outlook, 65
    PowerPoint document for review, 66
    review reminder, 167
embedding thumbnails, 95
embedding fonts, 156
exporting comments, 172
extracting pages, 103

F

File Attachment tool, 150
File attachment comments, 136, 150
File menu
    Acrobat 6, 70
    Adobe Reader, 10
File toolbar (Acrobat 6), 69
Fill color options, 153, 156
Filling in form fields and signing, allowing, 218
Fit in Window magnification level, 92
Fit Page, magnification level, 18
Fit Visible magnification level, 18
Fit Width magnification level, 18
Follow Articles cursor, 118
font
    checking (Adobe Reader), 27
    in header and footer, 79
    listing all, 91, 156
    size, 156
footers/headers. *See* headers/footers
Forms preferences (Adobe Reader), 28
Full Screen mode, 15, 120–121
    Adobe Reader, 15, 28
    navigation options, 120
    preferences, 120
Full Search feature, eBook Reader, 42

G

General eBookstores, 46–47
General preferences (Adobe Reader), 29
Go to Page dialog box (Adobe Reader), 21

H

Hand tool, 125
    Basic toolbar (Adobe Reader), 20
    switching temporarily, 20
headers/footers
    adding, 80
    editing, 81
    Headers and Footers dialog box, 79
    removing/restoring, 81
Help (Acrobat 6)
    Contents, 202–203
    Help file, 202
    Help menus
        Adobe 6, 71, 201
        Adobe Reader, 10
    Help pane, 202
    Index, 204
    menu options, 207–209
    printing Help topics, 206
    Search, 205
Hide All Comments option, 157
Hide window controls option, 93
Highlight button (eBook Reader), 51
Highlight Selected Text option, 140
Highlighting tool, 135, 154
    changing highlight color, 154
    eBook Reader, 51
Horizontal Scale option, 156
horizontal tiling, 19
How To pane, 68, 165, 210–212
How To Picture Tasks, 37
HTML Conversion settings, 61
HTML files, 56, 84

INDEX

INDEX

INDEX

Update preferences (Adobe Reader), 29
Updates option, 207

V

vertical tiling, 19
View menu
    Adobe 6, 70
    Adobe Reader, 10
viewing in Adobe Reader
    facing pages, 15
    PDF documents, 15
visibility, 223

W

watermarks, adding, 82–83
WAV files, 143
Web browsers, PDF documents/files
    adding comments to online, 198
    editing online, 198
    reviewing, 168
    setting to read, 197
    viewing, 197
Web Capture preferences, 129
Web Capture settings panel (Acrobat 6), 62
Web links
    adding for Adobe Reader 6 download, 131
    creating, 124–126
    creating, automatically, 127
    deleting, 131

    following, 129
    opening, 62
    setting appearances, 131
    setting properties, 128
Web Page Capture settings, 60
Web-based installation, 4–5
Window menu
    Adobe 6, 71
    Adobe Reader, 10
window view, splitting, 77
Windows
    Help menu, 201, 208–209
    installing Adobe Reader, 4–5
    setting up printing, 88
Word files (Microsoft), 56, 85
Word Spacing option, 156

X

XML and XML Data Package Files, 85

Z

Zoom In/Zoom out buttons
    Acrobat 6, 76
    Adobe Reader, 16
Zoom pop-up menu, 125
Zoom toolbar
    Acrobat 6, 76
    Adobe Reader, 7–8, 18

INDEX

WWW.PEACHPIT.COM

Quality How-to Computer Books

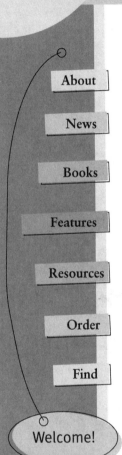

About

News

Books

Features

Resources

Order

Find

Welcome!

Visit Peachpit Press on the Web at www.peachpit.com

- Check out new feature articles each Monday: excerpts, interviews, tips, and plenty of how-tos

- Find any Peachpit book by title, series, author, or topic on the Books page

- See what our authors are up to on the News page: signings, chats, appearances, and more

- Meet the Peachpit staff and authors in the About section: bios, profiles, and candid shots

- Use Resources to reach our academic, sales, customer service, and tech support areas and find out how to become a Peachpit author

Peachpit.com is also the place to:

- Chat with our authors online
- Take advantage of special Web-only offers
- Get the latest info on new books